VESUVIUS

AND OTHER LATIN PLAYS

Dick Burnell

CAMBRIDGE
UNIVERSITY PRESS

PUBLISHED BY THE PRESS SYNDICATE OF THE UNIVERSITY OF CAMBRIDGE
The Pitt Building, Trumpington Street, Cambridge CB2 1RP, United Kingdom

CAMBRIDGE UNIVERSITY PRESS
The Edinburgh Building, Cambridge CB2 2RU, United Kingdom
40 West 20th Street, New York, NY 10011–4211, USA
10 Stamford Road, Oakleigh, Melbourne 3166, Australia

© Cambridge University Press 1991

First published 1991
Reprinted 1997

Printed in the United Kingdom at the University Press, Cambridge

A catalogue record for this book is available from the British Library

Library of Congress Cataloguing in Publication data

Burnell, Dick.
   Vesuvius and other Latin plays/Dick Burnell.
      p. cm.
   ISBN 0-521-40959-4
   1. Latin drama. Medieval and modern. 2. Latin language – Readers.
I. Title.
PA8485.B68V47   1991   90-26918
872'.0308 – dc20   CIP

ISBN 0 521 40959 4

Book design by Claire Brodmann

Picture research by Callie Kendall

Notice to teachers
The contents of this book are in the copyright of Cambridge University Press.
Unauthorised copying of any of the pages is not only illegal but also goes against
the interests of the author.

   For authorised copying please check that your school has a licence (through
the local education authority) from the Copyright Licensing Agency which
enables you to copy small parts of the text in limited numbers.

DS

CONTENTS

INTRODUCTION

These Latin plays were first put together in Britain for a play competition in East Anglia which we called *Ludi Scaenici*. The aim was to perform short plays in simple Latin for an audience that was made up of the other competitors. All those involved would be in their first year of Latin learning.

The plays had to use simple Latin. Several of the groups involved were using the Cambridge Latin Course, so the rules stated that the language and the situations had to be comprehensible to pupils who had completed Unit I of CLC. *volō*, *nōlō* and *possum* + infinitive were allowed and very much increased the possibilities. In performance the plays were intended to last only five minutes. Ideas at least, and often much more, were suggested by pupils, although most group teachers would admit to some input.

Why publish plays like this in book form? Firstly, because we enjoyed making them, dressing up, learning lines, rehearsing business, even performing. Secondly, to show how easy it is. Try it! Thirdly, to suggest that speaking Latin is a good way of learning to master the language, and a play provides better material for a group to speak, than individual recitation-pieces.

Thanks are due to CLC and its original writers who provided so rich a fund of ideas, and demonstrated exceptionally well the art of simple story-telling with a limited vocabulary. Thanks also to the teachers and schools whose plays are presented here, that they have so willingly made the material available:

Colne High School
Copleston High School, Ipswich
Ipswich School
Norwich High School
Paston School, North Walsham
St Felix School, Southwold

Finally thanks to all in East Anglian Joint Association of Classical Teachers who have helped to stage *Ludi Scaenici* over a dozen years, and the many pupils who have taken part. It seems they enjoy the memory.

ACKNOWLEDGEMENTS

The author and publisher would like to thank the following for permission to reproduce photographs: p.39 Reproduced by courtesy of the Trustees of the British Museum; p.51 The Mansell Collection; p.73 Reproduced by courtesy of the Trustees of the British Museum.

STAGE DIRECTIONS

There are two kinds of directions in this playscript. Those in **bold type** provide information that is essential to an understanding of what is happening in the play at that time. For a play-reading, these should be read by a separate reader.

Those in *italic type* are less essential stage directions and offer suggestions to assist with a production of the play on stage. In a reading they are best not read out as they will hamper the flow of the play, although those who are reading may find that some of these instructions offer help with the interpretation of their lines.

STATUES

INTRODUCTION

In many Roman houses the master showed his wealth and good taste by decorating rooms and gardens with works of art—both Greek originals and, more often, copies.

In *Statues* the master has taken his enthusiasm for his statues too far. His slave dusts and polishes them like sacred objects, while the master ignores his wife and children. Their plot to punish him is successful.

CHARACTERS

MAXIMUS, the master
RUFUS, a slave of Maximus
ANTONIA, wife of Maximus
MARCUS, elder son of Maximus
ANTONILLA, daughter of Maximus
SECUNDUS, younger son of Maximus
FOUR "STATUES" (non-speaking)

The scene is a room in a Roman house. Four STATUES are lined up: there is a HEROINE wielding a knife; a HERCULES carrying a club; a YOUNG GIRL holding an apple, and a SMALL BOY posed like a famous orator. RUFUS, a slave, is kneeling before them, dusting and polishing.

RUFUS   dominus meus statuās habet. statuās multās habet. statuae dominum dēlectant. statuae sunt pulchrae. statuae sunt pretiōsae. sed dominus est stultissimus. dominus statuās adōrat. deī igitur sunt īrātī, larēs sunt īrātī quod dominus statuās adōrat.

MAXIMUS   (*off stage*) Rūfe, venī hūc!

adōrat   *worships*

RUFUS	(*He hears the order but takes no notice.*) ēheu! dominus mē vocat.

Enter ANTONIA.

ANTONIA	dominus est vir meus, Maximus. ego sum uxor, Antōnia. Maximus tamen mē nōn amat. statuās amat. multam pecūniam non habēmus. multum cibum nōn habēmus. paucōs servōs habēmus, quod multās statuās habēmus. ēheu!

ANTONIA **stands aside. Her son,** MARCUS, **enters.**

MARCUS	dominus est pater meus. ego sum fīlius, Marcus. sed ego in forō cum patre nōn labōrō. ego ad thermās cum patre nōn ambulō. pater statuās adōrat. multās statuās habet.

He turns on RUFUS **who is still working.**

quid agis? statuāsne cūrās? ēheu!

He stands aside as ANTONILLA **enters.**

MAXIMUS	(*off stage*) serve, venī hūc celeriter!
RUFUS	ēheu! dominus me vocat.
ANTONILLA	dominus est pater meus. ego sum fīlia, Antōnilla. pater mē nōn amat. pater mihi virum nōn quaerit. pater semper statuās amat. ego igitur virum nōn habeō. mox senēscō.

She turns on RUFUS.

quid agis? semperne statuās cūrās? ēheu!

She stands aside as SECUNDUS, **her younger brother enters.**

MAXIMUS	(*off stage*) Rūfe, venī hūc celerrimē!
RUFUS	ēheu! dominus mē vocat.
SECUNDUS	dominus est pater meus, Maximus. ego sum parvus fīlius. pater mē nōn amat. pater mēcum nōn lūdit. pater mē nōn videt. pater statuās habet et spectat.

vir	*husband*	celerrimē	*very quickly*
senēscō	*grow old*	lūdit	*plays*

He turns to RUFUS.

> quid agis?

RUFUS, **kneeling to polish the feet of the statues, looks as if he might be worshipping.**

> adōrāsne statuās? ēheu! ubi est cibus? cibus nōn adest.

ANTONILLA ubi est vir? nōn adest vir.

MARCUS ubi est pater?

ANTONIA ubi est vir meus?

ALL (*together*) ēheu!

The members of the FAMILY **are now standing together at one side of the stage, so that the audience no longer notices them.** MAXIMUS **enters. He does not notice his family.**

MAXIMUS ego sum dominus, Maximus. ego statuās habeō. statuās habeō multās et pulchrās. statuae sunt pretiōsae. pecūniam nōn habeō. cibum nōn habeō. amīcōs nōn habeō. sed multās et pulchrās statuās habeō. Rūfe, venī hūc!

RUFUS **goes over to** MAXIMUS **who points out the statues, explaining enthusiastically what he likes about them. He points at 'Hercules'.**

> haec statua est validior quam fīlius meus.

He points at the knife-wielding heroine.

> ecce! haec statua est pulchrior quam uxor mea.

He points at the girl and boy statues.

> hae statuae sunt dulciōrēs quam līberī meī.

RUFUS ēheu!

MAXIMUS nunc fessus sum.

MAXIMUS **curls up to sleep on a convenient couch. The** FAMILY **move forward. Like conspirators they mutter together resentfully.**

ubi?	*where?*	dulciōrēs	*dearer*
validior	*stronger*	fessus	*tired*

ANTONIA   statuae mē nōn dēlectant.

MARCUS   statuae mē nōn dēlectant.

ANTONILLA   statuae mē nōn dēlectant.

SECUNDUS **simply wails.**

ANTONIA   iam vir meus poenam dat.

MARCUS   iam pater meus poenam dat. iam pecūniam habeō.

ANTONILLA   iam pater poenam dat. iam virum habeō.

SECUNDUS   iam pater poenam dat. iam cibum habeō.

The FAMILY put their heads together to finalise their plan. RUFUS addresses the audience.

RUFUS   iam dominus dormit. iam statuās videt. iam statuae eum
             dēlectant. sed deī sunt īrātī. larēs sunt īrātī. uxor et fīlia sunt
             īrātae. fīliī sunt īrātī. ēheu!

ANTONIA, ANTONILLA, MARCUS and SECUNDUS take each of the statues in turn, and topple them over. ANTONIA takes the heroine's knife, MARCUS takes Hercules' club, ANTONILLA takes the girl's apple, and SECUNDUS takes the pose of the orator. They take the places of the statues that have been moved and stand quite still. Now they try to wake MAXIMUS up. Each makes a noise in turn.

ANTONIA   ah! ah!

RUFUS hasn't noticed what has been going on, and is puzzled by the noise.

RUFUS   quid est? uxor ululāvit. quid est?

MARCUS   ah! ah!

RUFUS   quid est? Mārcus clāmāvit. quid est?

ANTONILLA   ah! ah!

RUFUS   quid est? fīlia lacrimāvit. quid est?

SECUNDUS   ah! ah!

RUFUS   quid est? parvus fīlius, Secundus, vāgīvit. quid est?

             poenam dat   *pays the penalty, gets what he deserves*
             vāgīvit   *cried*

Confused, RUFUS goes off in search of the family. Meanwhile MAXIMUS must have heard the cries. He wakes up. But he is puzzled and half-asleep.

> MAXIMUS   quid est? quid audīvī? quid sēnsī? num quid accidit? omnēsne sunt tūtae?

His first thought is for his statues. He goes to look at them, but doesn't notice the change.

> statuae meae. omnēs sunt tūtae.

MAXIMUS stands with his back to the statues, like a proprietor standing before his shop, or a champion before his trophies. ANTONILLA tweaks his hair and makes him turn suddenly, but by the time he looks round there is no movement. SECUNDUS taps his shoulder. When he looks one way, the tap comes on his other shoulder. The children play him along, until ANTONIA, who has been imitating the knife-wielding heroine, brings the knife down on him. He calls for help.

> ēheu! quid est? uxor, venī! nōn vēnit. ubi est? non adest. līberī, venīte! non vēnērunt. non adsunt. Rūfe, venī! vēnī hūc quam celerrimē! familiam quaerō. (*looking around*) familiam non inveniō.

At this moment he catches sight of MARCUS, who has been posing as Hercules, just as he brings down his club on his father's head.

> statuae sunt vīvae!

MAXIMUS collapses. At this the FAMILY come down to him and show some, but not too much, concern.

> ANTONILLA   estne mortuus?
>
> ANTONIA   minimē. aeger est.
>
> MARCUS   est exanimātus.
>
> ANTONIA   ubi est medicus?
>
> MARCUS   nōn adest medicus.
>
> ANTONILLA   mortuus est. ego timeō.

num quid?	(*has*) *anything?*	estne?	*is he?*
vīvae	*alive*	medicus	*doctor*

MAXIMUS **stirs, and the** FAMILY **resume their motionless postures. He raises his head, and in time-honoured fashion . . .**

> MAXIMUS   ēheu! ubi sum? mortuusne sum?

MAXIMUS **staggers to his feet and sees the 'statues'. The sight is too much.**

> statuae! ego statuās timeō. ō familia mea! ubi est familia?
> Antōnia, uxor mea! uxor mea pulchrior erat quam lūna.
> Mārcus, fīlius meus! fīlius meus validior erat quam leō. līberī
> meī! ubi sunt? Rūfe, venī hūc!

RUFUS **comes forward.**

> statuae!

MAXIMUS **takes a last disgusted look at the statues.**

> ēheu! Rūfe, dēice! dēlē! frange!

MAXIMUS **turns away as** RUFUS **sets about taking down the 'statues'.** RUFUS **double-takes as they move and show themselves to be flesh and blood. The** FAMILY **line up behind the unaware** MAXIMUS.

> MAXIMUS   ubi est familia? familiam quaerō.

At this point the FAMILY **surges over him, with cries of** "euge!" "ecce!" "hīc

> adsum!"

The final picture is of the happy, forgiven, and—one hopes—forgiving father, surrounded by his family.

dēice!	*throw down!*	frange!	*break!*
dēlē!	*destroy!*	hīc	*here*

A NOTE TO THE PRODUCER

This play depends on the skill of four non-speaking actors who have to convince the audience that they really are statues. They must match as closely as possible the four family actors who take their places. Perhaps a dusting of powder will help them look like marble statues.

In one past performance the statues were able to hold their pose so stiffly that a member of the audience was heard to say, "I thought they were only actors, *until they were carried off.*"

PROPS

To provide, find, improvise or imagine.

Each of the STATUES has a recognisable token: Hercules' club, a heroine's knife, the girl's apple, which the family can use to distract or harm Maximus.

RUFUS needs "cleaning equipment".

GOING HOME

INTRODUCTION

Two faithful slaves follow their drunken master home late at night through the dangerous, dark streets of Pompeii. The dangers of the streets of Rome, including the bully-boy attendants of very rich men (perhaps the emperor himself!) are mentioned by the Roman poet Juvenal. The traveller might meet robbers at any time, but the man with no money at all could whistle in their faces!

CHARACTERS

CAECILIUS
TWO SLAVES
TWO THIEVES
BEGGAR
HUGE MAN (it may be necessary to put one actor on
            another's shoulders) a non-speaking part
RICH MAN (voice only)
LITTER BEARERS (4, 6, or 8, depending on the size of the
            litter)
METELLA, Caecilius' wife

The scene is a street in Pompeii, with two doors, some distance apart. TWO THIEVES are already lurking in a dark corner. CAECILIUS appears from one of the doors. He is leaving a friend's house. He is dressed in a tunic and his hands are full of bits and pieces. As he appears, TWO SLAVES follow him and pick up each thing he drops as he drops it. SLAVE I is carrying a folded toga.

CAECILIUS	nunc ad vīllam prōcēdō.
SLAVE I	(*quietly*) ēbrius est.

CAECILIUS **hears him.**

CAECILIUS   minimē. hilaris sum, ēbrius nōn sum. serve, venī hūc!
togam mihi da.

SLAVE 1 **gives him the toga all in a heap.**

ēheu! eam compōne!

The SLAVES **help him into his toga. He shouts a last good-bye to his friend.**

iam . . . valē! valē, amīce!

He sets out followed by the SLAVES. **He seems to be taking a roundabout route.**

tandem ad vīllam meam veniō. ēheu! nox est obscūra.

Meanwhile the TWO THIEVES **are preparing for a night of activity. Each is
carrying a club.**

THIEF 1   euge! nox est obscūra. fūstemne habēs?

THIEF 2   ita vērō. fūstem habeō.

THIEF 1   ego quoque fūstem habeō. nunc cīvēs dīvitēs quaerimus.

THIEF 2   nunc pecūniam quaerimus.

THIEF 1   ita vērō. dēnāriōs. nunc dēnāriōs petimus. ecce! sonum
audīvī.

He has probably heard CAECILIUS **who is still some distance away.**

audīvistīnc tū quoque sonum? tacē!

CAECILIUS **moves away from his friend's house. A** BEGGAR **enters and approaches
him.**

BEGGAR   salvē, domine!

CAECILIUS   salvē, pauper! quid cupis?

The BEGGAR **goes into his routine.**

BEGGAR   ego habeō nūllam pecūniam. līberōs multōs habeō. uxōrem
aegram habeō. nūllam togam habeō.

CAECILIUS   nūllam togam? ēheu! miser es, nēmō miserior.
miserrimus es.

| hilaris | *cheerful* | | miser | *miserable* |
| eam | *it* | | *also* miserior, miserrimus | |

BEGGAR	valdē pauper sum, nēmō pauperior. pauperrimus sum.
CAECILIUS	ecce! togam tibi dō.

The BEGGAR **wants money. He doesn't really want a toga!**

BEGGAR	minimē.
CAECILIUS	(*insisting*) ita vērō.
BEGGAR	sed . . .

The SLAVES **arrange** CAECILIUS' **toga on the** BEGGAR.

grātiās tibi agō.

The BEGGAR **goes off wearing the toga, proud but also disappointed. As he goes,** CAECILIUS **shouts after him.**

CAECILIUS	pulcherrimus es et togam pulcherrimam geris.

Meanwhile, the THIEVES **are still looking out for a possible victim.**

THIEF I	tacē! . . . sonum . . .

There is the sound of singing, and a man rattling his money.

est dīves. pecūniam habet. dēnāriōs audiō.

A HUGE MAN **appears.**

THIEF 2	ēheu! ingēns est.
THIEF I	est ingentissimus.
THIEF 2	timeō.
THIEF I	ego quoque.

The HUGE MAN **passes the cowering** THIEVES **and exits.**

THIEF 2	ubi est dīves?
THIEF I	exspectā. dīvitem quaerimus.

The THIEVES **crouch again. Meanwhile** CAECILIUS **wanders past, but not close enough for the** THIEVES. **He thinks he notices a cat.**

CAECILIUS	fēlem videō.

CAECILIUS **drops something that he is carrying. The** SLAVES **pause to pick it up, so that for a moment** CAECILIUS **moves away from their protection.**

> ubi est fēlēs? fēlēs! s-s-suāvissima.

CAECILIUS **is heading towards the** THIEVES, **who raise their clubs. At last the** SLAVES **notice that** CAECILIUS **has moved away from them.**

SLAVE 2   discēdit . . . discessit!

SLAVE I   revenī!

SLAVE 2   revenī, domine!

The SLAVES **catch up with** CAECILIUS **and point him in a different direction. Now he is out of the** THIEVES' **reach! Suddenly the** THIEVES **get themselves ready again. There is a commotion off-stage.**

THIEF I   ecce! clāmōrem audiō. fūstem parā!

THIEF 2   eum parāvī. parātus est.

THIEF I   tacē!

A RICH MAN's **litter and** BEARERS **suddenly speed across the scene, carrying torches, etc. It might even be the emperor after a night out! The** THIEVES **are poised ready to swing their clubs, but freeze in their position. There is an aristocratic voice from inside the closed litter.**

RICH MAN   (*voice only*) quam celerrimē!

THIEF 2   (*impressed*) quis erat?

THIEF I   (*equally impressed*) eratne . . .?

THIEF 2   (*echoing*) eratne . . .?

THIEF I   ipse!

CAECILIUS **has also noticed the great man.**

CAECILIUS   (*amazed*) eratne ipse? ipsum vīdī . . . per nostrās viās ipse prōcēdēbat!

CAECILIUS **backs towards the** THIEVES, **who swing their clubs back again. The** SLAVES **are still worried about their master.**

suāvissima	*sweetest*	ipse	*(the great man) himself*
eum	*it*		

SLAVE 1   revenī!

SLAVE 2   venī hūc!

CAECILIUS **now, at the vital moment, realises that he has been without his toga for too long. He moves away.**

CAECILIUS   (*shivering*) ēheu! frīgidus sum.

The THIEVES **are still looking for action. Is there another lonely traveller?**

THIEF 1   sshhh!!

Enter the BEGGAR. **He is still well wrapped up in Caecilius' toga, and is carrying a tiny candle. As the** THIEVES **swing their clubs back, he seems to see them, and greets them cheerily.**

BEGGAR   salvēte, fūrēs!

THIEF 2   salvē, frāter! (*Fingering the toga*) quid est hoc?

BEGGAR   est toga.

THIEF 1   est toga splendida. bene tū fēcistī!

As the BEGGAR **goes off,** CAECILIUS **wanders towards the** THIEVES **again. The** THIEVES **get ready.** THIEF 1 **takes charge. This is going to be the big one!**

THIEF 1   iterum tacē!

CAECILIUS   tandem ad vīllam veniō. nunc tūtus ad vīllam . . . brrr.

CAECILIUS **shivers and the things in his hands drop everywhere. The** SLAVES **gather them, and pile them up.** THIEF 2 **swings his club back.**

THIEF 1   tenē! exspectā!

THIEF 2   iam?

THIEF 1   minimē.

THIEF 2   iam?

THIEF 1   minimē.

CAECILIUS **keeps dropping things, and his** SLAVES **can't keep up with him. They**

frīgidus   *cold*   bene   *well*

have their hands full. CAECILIUS goes off alone, and the THIEVES move in, one on each side. They swing back their clubs to flatten him, but he has dropped something. As he bends down to pick it up himself . . .

    THIEF 1   nunc!

The THIEVES lash out at him from both sides. Over his head, they knock each other out.

    SLAVE 1   fūrēs!

    SLAVE 2   scelerātī!

The SLAVES grab the dazed THIEVES and drag them off, under arrest.

    SLAVE 1   venīte!

CAECILIUS is now on his own, and has at last reached his own front-door.

    CAECILIUS   haec est iānua mea. tandem ad vīllam veniō. iānuam pulsō.

CAECILIUS knocks. METELLA answers the door.

    METELLA   ecce! tandem vēnistī! hoc recipe!

METELLA wields a rolling-pin and strikes CAECILIUS.

    CAECILIUS   ēheu!

scelerātī   *crooks!*   recipe   *take*

A NOTE TO THE PRODUCER

This play needs as much space as can be allowed, and several apparent hiding-places. If there really is not much room, the actors must give each other space by "freezing", and must make the audience believe that characters who are hiding cannot be seen. Caecilius' wanderings are likely to take him very near other characters whom he must not notice.

Clearly much of this is knockabout comedy, and the Beggar can be played as a cheery comic figure. One of the secrets of successful comedy is to get the details right, and it will take a lot of careful rehearsal for the two Slaves to be able to drape a toga convincingly.

PROPS

To provide, find, improvise or imagine.

For once, an item of costume is a vital prop: the SLAVES must carry a toga, which they put on Caecilius and later put on the Beggar.

CAECILIUS is carrying various small items which he drops, and which the Slaves pick up for him.

THIEVES   two clubs

HUGE MAN   a rattling purse of money

RICH MAN and his LITTER BEARERS   a litter: a two-dimensional litter with the curtain drawn. Torches need to be attached.

BEGGAR   small candle

METELLA   rolling-pin.

AT THE RHETOR'S

INTRODUCTION

The rhetor prepared boys for public life where speechmaking at public meetings or in court was important for success. The image-makers and TV coaches of the modern political world carry out a comparable role. The pupils practised their debating skills by making speeches to the teacher and to each other. In this play, the Roman children resent the Greek teacher's favourite Greek pupil, and plot to cause his downfall.

The Roman empire included vast numbers of people of different racial backgrounds. In Pompeii, Greek words were written on the walls, alongside Latin, sometimes in the Greek alphabet, sometimes in Roman letters. The poet Juvenal, in his *Satires*, expresses a Roman's resentment against the success of the immigrant Greek race. It is not certain whether many Romans agreed with him.

CHARACTERS

ALEXANDER, a Greek pupil
QUINTUS
MARCUS
LUCIUS   } Roman pupils
GAIUS
Other, non-speaking PUPILS
The RHETOR, Theodorus

The action takes place where a Roman teacher would hold his class—not a modern schoolroom, but a room in a house perhaps, a corner of a garden, or even a street.

Enter ALEXANDER, QUINTUS, MARCUS, LUCIUS, GAIUS **with other (non-speaking)**

Roman pupils, if required. The ROMAN BOYS **form a group separate from**
ALEXANDER.

ALEXANDER	Graecī sunt optimī. ego Graecus sum. ego sum optimus.
QUINTUS	quam superbus Alexander est, quod herī in contrōversiā mē vīcit.
MARCUS	hercle! ego eum nōn amō. nōs Rōmānī sumus meliōrēs quam Graecī.
LUCIUS	ita vērō. Theodōrus, rhētor noster, stultissimus est. Alexandrum maximē amat quod Graecus Graecum amat.
GAIUS	ēheu! Alexander in contrōversiīs semper vincit, quod Graecōs semper laudat et nōs Rōmānōs semper vituperat.
ALEXANDER	Graecī sunt auctōrēs. Rōmānī sunt imitātōrēs.
MARCUS	nūllōs Graecōs amō. nūllīs Graecīs crēdō. omnēs Graecī sunt pessimī.
QUINTUS	cōnsilium callidum habeō.

The ROMAN BOYS **gather round.**

	cūr Alexandrum nōn pūnīmus? ubi rhētor Alexandrum nōn amat, nōn iam Alexander in contrōversiīs vincit.
GAIUS	cōnsilium habēs? quid est? callidumne est? Graecī Graecōs semper amant.
QUINTUS	(*slowly*) rhētor . . . Alexandrum . . . verberat.
ROMAN BOYS	(*variously*) cūr? quō modō? caudex es!

Meanwhile, ALEXANDER **arranges his writing equipment for the lesson, before
starting to show off.**

ALEXANDER	nōs Graecī semper meliōrēs sumus. nōs sumus auctōrēs, nōs sumus . . .

superbus	*proud*	pūnīmus	*we punish*
vīcit	*defeated*	ubi	*when*
maximē	*very much, most*	quō modō?	*how?*
vincit	*wins*		

LUCIUS   ecce! Alexander librum habet. Alexander cērās et stilōs
habet. Mārce et Quīnte, capite librum . . .

MARCUS **and** QUINTUS **steal the book . . .**

et cērās . . .

They steal the tablets . . .

et stilōs!

They steal the styluses. LUCIUS, GAIUS **and perhaps others pick a quarrel with**
ALEXANDER **and keep him occupied. Meanwhile** MARCUS **reads what** ALEXANDER
has written on the wax tablets.

MARCUS   (*reading*) "omnēs Rōmānī sunt stul . . . tiss . . . imī.
omnēs . . ."

GAIUS **takes a stylus and offers it to** MARCUS.

GAIUS   minimē. stilum cape. ērāde, Mārce. scrībe . . . "omnēs
Graecī sunt stultissimī."

QUINTUS   trāde mihi cērās!

QUINTUS **grabs the wax tablets and stylus and by using the reverse flat end erases**
some words. Then with the sharp end he writes something else. The RHETOR
enters.

RHETOR   tacēte, puerī. sedēte. cūr cum Alexandrō semper pugnātis?
vōs Rōmānī estis semper pugnācēs. Alexander est optimus
discipulus. Alexander . . .

ALEXANDER **has managed to get back his writing equipment.**

Alexander, dā mihi illās cērās.

The RHETOR **takes** ALEXANDER**'s tablets and reads, aloud of course.**

"Mārcus et Quīntus sunt Rōmānī. omnēs Rōmānī sunt
stultī." (*He laughs.*) ita vērō "Mārcus et Quīntus dīligenter
nōn labōrant. Mārcus et Quīntus . . ." (*As he reads on he*
becomes more thoughtful.) "rhētor est caudex. rhētor est
stultissimus. omnēs Graecī sunt stultissimī." Alexander, cūr
tū illa scrībis? cūr . . . ?

pugnācēs   *ready for a fight*   discipulus   *pupil*

ALEXANDER   sed . . . sed . . . ego . . . nōn . . .

RHETOR   Alexander, tē iam pūniō. iam Graecus tē Graecum nōn amō. iam tē verberō.

The RHETOR **grabs** ALEXANDER **and beats him till he howls. The** ROMAN BOYS **meanwhile congratulate each other.**

QUINTUS   nōs Rōmānī nōn semper sumus stultissimī.

MARCUS   nōs quoque callidissima cōnsilia habēmus.

LUCIUS   nōs Rōmānī sumus auctōrēs. nōs Rōmānī Alexandrum pūnīmus.

GAIUS   hodiē certē Alexander in contrōversiā nōn vincit.

The ROMAN BOYS **go off laughing.**

certē   *for sure*

A NOTE TO THE PRODUCER

Make sure your actors know how to *act* a fight. It needs a great deal of controlled movement, and apparent aggression. Be careful also to build up the Rhetor's position by insisting that all the pupils show a nervous respect. He will only be convincing if *they* convince the audience.

PROPS

To provide, find, improvise or imagine.

Each of the BOYS needs school equipment: it will include papyrus rolls, wax tablets and styluses, perhaps in the correct equipment-box, *capsa*.

The RHETOR needs a cane.

THE CRUEL SCHOOLMASTER

INTRODUCTION

Roman teachers were all male—men of low class, perhaps freedmen—who had a reputation for brutality. Most pupils also were boys. But this should not stop female actors taking part.

In this play, the master is cruel, the pupils are aggressive, and the end of the story is savage.

CHARACTERS

TEACHER
GHOST
and eight boys, who conveniently have the names of Roman ordinal numbers:
PRIMUS
SECUNDUS
TERTIUS
QUARTUS
QUINTUS
SEXTUS
SEPTIMUS
OCTAVUS

The action takes place where a Roman teacher would hold his class—a room in a house or a space outside.

Three boys, PRIMUS, SECUNDUS and TERTIUS enter.

PRIMUS   lūdus mē nōn dēlectat. ad lūdum īre nōlō.

lūdus	school		nōlō	I don't want
īre	to go			

SECUNDUS   odiōsus est magister. semper labōrāmus.

TERTIUS   crūdēlis est magister. nōs semper verberat.

PRIMUS and SECUNDUS examine old scars.

PRIMUS   ita vērō.

Four more boys, QUARTUS, QUINTUS, SEXTUS and SEPTIMUS enter.

QUARTUS   salvēte, omnēs.

QUARTUS greets QUINTUS who follows him in.

salvē, Quīnte.

QUARTUS and QUINTUS settle down to a game of knucklebones.

TERTIUS   salvēte, pestēs. quid agitis?

QUINTUS   tū quoque pestis.

A fight develops between TERTIUS and the rest. The TEACHER enters.

SEXTUS   cavēte, omnēs! magister adest.

TEACHER   (*savagely*) tacēte, omnēs! quid facitis? hic est lūdus, nōn arēna. vōsne bēstiae estis?

The TEACHER brandishes a whip.

gladiātōrēs bēstiās necant. ego gladium nōn habeō . . . sed virgas habeō.

The BOYS cower.

sedēte, omnēs puerī.

The BOYS scuttle back to their seats. The TEACHER glowers at them.

audīte mē. heri vōbīs fābulam dē urbe Troiā nārrāvī. hodiē vōs mihi fābulam nārrāte. Septime, tū prīmus.

SEPTIMUS stands up.

odiōsus	*hateful*	quid agitis?	*how are you?*
magister	*teacher (of young children)*	cavēte	*beware*
crūdēlis	*cruel*	virgas	*a bundle of rods (for beating)*

SEPTIMUS   (*hesitantly*) Graecī et Troiānī inimīcī erant. Graecī ad urbem nāvigāvērunt. longum erat bellum. tandem Graecī urbem intrāvērunt. omnēs vīllas dēlēvērunt, omnēs Troiānōs . . .

Suddenly OCTAVUS **enters.**

SEXTUS   Octāve, quid est?

OCTAVUS   magister, magister!

TEACHER   ō puer pessime, cūr tardus vēnistī?

OCTAVUS   ad lūdum festīnābam. per viam currēbam quod tardus eram. subitō rem mīrābilem vīdī. umbram vīdī.

The BOYS **gasp. The** TEACHER **looks threateningly.**

vērum dīcō, magister. erat umbra. umbra mē petīvit. umbra mē terret. ego hūc quam celerrimē contendī.

TEACHER   furcifer! tū umbram nōn vīdistī. nunc ego tē verberō.

The TEACHER **seizes** OCTAVUS **by his tunic. As he raises his whip, the** GHOST **enters. Its face is white and strange. It moves in a slow and frightening manner. The** BOYS **shriek.**

BOYS   (*variously*) umbra est! ēheu! quis est? timeō!

The GHOST **approaches the** TEACHER**.**

SEXTUS   hanc umbram agnōscō. est Pūblius. Pūblius est mortuus. tū Pūblium verberāvistī. tū Pūblium necāvistī.

The TEACHER **yells as the** GHOST **advances on him, and seizes the whip. The** BOYS **circle round and drag the** TEACHER **down to the floor. The** GHOST **flogs the** TEACHER **in slow motion, and the** BOYS **chant, like the crowd in the arena.**

BOYS   (*variously*) verberā! ūre! habet!

Finally, the BOYS **exuent, leaving the** GHOST **standing over the body of the** TEACHER**. The** GHOST **circles the body slowly, and slowly exits as the light fades.**

nāvigāvērunt	*sailed*	ūre	*burn (him)*
bellum	*war*	habet	*he has it (the blow)* = *take that!*
tardus	*late*		(the cry of the crowd at the
vērum	*truth*		games)

A NOTE TO THE PRODUCER

The final actions of the play require great discipline from the actors who (probably) should enact the violence in a slow ritual and a non-realistic manner. If the lighting can be controlled it may be possible to provide an ending of real horror.

PROPS

To provide, find, improvise or imagine.

The BOYS should have school equipment—papyrus, wax tablets and styluses. They may have other things, especially knucklebones to play with.

The TEACHER has a whip or bundle of sticks (which he calls *virgae*).

POISONER

INTRODUCTION

Congrio and Domitilla, slaves in the house, are plotting to gain their freedom. Only when they become "ex-slaves" can they marry and live independently. Their master shows no sign of freeing them in his lifetime, but he can set them free in his will.

Poison was a popular topic in the scandalous gossip of Rome. No doubt many did die of accidental food-poisoning or infections (or, for example, appendicitis) which now would receive effective medical treatment. According to the gossip-writers, many in the Imperial family, and even some emperors, died of poison!

CHARACTERS

DOMITILLA, a slave girl
CONGRIO, a slave
LURCIO, a cook
MEGADORUS, the master
TRANIO ⎫
ANTHRAX ⎬ non-speaking slaves
BALLIO ⎭

Enter DOMITILLA, **a slave girl, with an urn of water. She starts scrubbing the floor.** CONGRIO, **a slave, enters. He runs up quickly and taps her on the shoulder.**

DOMITILLA ō Congrio, dēliciae meae!

CONGRIO Domitilla, quam fēlīx sum! tū es mea columba.

DOMITILLA tū quoque es suspīrium meum. ego tē amō.

CONGRIO et ego tē amō. sed vīta est dūra. ego sum servus.

DOMITILLA (*sadly*) et ego sum ancilla.

CONGRIO (*angrily*) et dominum pessimum habēmus. dominus mē vexat, quod mē nōn līberāvit. ego tē in mātrimōnium dūcere cupiō . . .

DOMITILLA ō Congrio!

CONGRIO sed dominus nōn cupit. dominus mē līberāre nōn cupit. sed dominus est senex. testāmentum hodiē fēcit.

DOMITILLA (*surprised*) testāmentum fēcit?

CONGRIO ita vērō. ego testāmentum vīdī. ubi dominus mortuus est, nōs sumus lībertī.

DOMITILLA quam misera sum!

There is a pause.

CONGRIO Domitilla, ego cōnsilium habeō. audī! nōnne dominus nunc in thermīs est?

DOMITILLA ita vērō. in thermīs est. mox ad vīllam revenit.

CONGRIO ubi vīllam intrat, nōnne vīnum semper bibit?

DOMITILLA ita vērō. vīnum semper bibit. vīnum dominum dēlectat.

CONGRIO bene. ego dominō pōculum dō. sed in pōculō est venēnum!

DOMITILLA (*shocked*) in pōculō? . . . venēnum?! sed perīculōsum est.

CONGRIO minimē. dominus vīnum bibit.

CONGRIO **mimes the actions and the result.**

suspīrium	*heart-throb*	misera	*wretched*
dūra	*hard*	nōnne . . . est?	*he is, isn't he?*
in mātrimōnium dūcere	*to marry*	nōnne . . . (bibit)?	*(he does), doesn't he?*
testāmentum	*will*	bene	*good*
ubi	*when*	venēnum	*poison*

> dominus mortuus prōcumbit. nōs sumus lībertī. ego tē in
> mātrimōnium dūcō.

**Meanwhile, LURCIO the cook enters. He is carrying a bowl which he is stirring
with a spoon. LURCIO is not very bright.**

DOMITILLA   cōnsilium est optimum.

CONGRIO   Lurcio, hūc venī! ubi est vīnum? fer mihi pōcula!

CONGRIO produces a small flask.

> in ūnō pōculō pōne hoc! hoc est venēnum.

LURCIO gasps.

> dominus pōculum haurit. tum dominus mortuus est.

**LURCIO takes the flask muttering anxiously. But before he can exit, MEGADORUS
enters, followed by three very scared SLAVES. LURCIO moves aside.**

MEGADORUS   (*angrily*) caudicēs, venīte hūc! Trānio, stultissimus es. toga
mea est sordida. Anthrax, ego tē vituperō, quod ignāvus es.
portā hanc lacernam. (*He gives his cloak to Anthrax.*)
Ballio, ubi es? quaere Lurciōnem.

BALLIO brings LURCIO forward.

> Lurcio, ego quīnque amīcōs ad cēnam invītāvī.

LURCIO   quīnque!

MEGADORUS   nōs pāvōnem et ostreās cupimus. curre ad culīnam.

LURCIO runs out bewildered, muttering.

LURCIO   pāvōnem! ostreās!

MEGADORUS   ego nunc ad tablīnum eō. tum vīnum bibō.

**MEGADORUS and the SLAVES exeunt. After MEGADORUS has gone, CONGRIO shakes
his fist behind his master's back.**

prōcumbit	*falls flat*	haurit	*drains, drinks up*
ubi?	*where?*	lacernam	*cloak*
fer!	*bring, carry!*	ostreās	*oysters*
pōne	*put!*	eō	*I go*

CONGRIO   mox tū mortuus es, Megadōre! et tum ego sum lībertus.

CONGRIO **and** DOMITILLA **go out arm in arm.** LURCIO **enters with a tray bearing wine cups and the flask. He puts it down on the table.**

LURCIO   (*puzzled*) ēheu! quam trīstis sum! Congrio mihi dīxit, "pōne venēnum in ūnō pōculō." ego venēnum in pōculō posuī. sed ubi nunc est venēnum? in hōc pōculō?

LURCIO **picks up one cup.**

         an in hōc?

He picks up another.

         nesciō!

MEGADORUS   (*shouting off stage*) Congrio! Trānio! ubi est vīnum?

LURCIO   ēheu! venēnum iterum in pōculō pōnō.

LURCIO **adds poison to a cup.** MEGADORUS **enters in a rage, followed by** CONGRIO, **and** TRANIO. LURCIO **shows** CONGRIO **the cup in which he has just put the poison.**

MEGADORUS   ubi est vīnum? vīnum mē dēlectat.

MEGADORUS **spots** LURCIO.

         Lurcio, ad culīnam abī!

LURCIO **goes out hastily.** CONGRIO **offers the poisoned cup to** MEGADORUS.

CONGRIO   domine, vīnum optimum tibi offerō.

MEGADORUS   dā mihi! (*He drinks deeply.*) vīnum est opt . . .

The poison takes effect and MEGADORUS **dies.** TRANIO **exits screaming.** DOMITILLA **enters.**

DOMITILLA   ō dēliciae meae. mortuus est Megadōrus.

CONGRIO   Megadōrus est mortuus et ego sum lībertus.

CONGRIO **takes another cup from the tray.**

         Domitilla, nunc laetissimus sum.

an	*or*	abī	*go away!*
nesciō	*I don't know*		

He drinks to her. Then after a second or two, he grasps his stomach in agony.

Domitilla!

DOMITILLA   quid est?

CONGRIO   moribundus sum. ō Domitilla, vīta est dūra.

CONGRIO **dies.**

DOMITILLA   ō meum corculum! quid fēcistī? o quam īnfēlīx sum!

DOMITILLA **bursts into tears.** LURCIO **enters and sees** CONGRIO's **body and the tray. He looks puzzled, then guilty, and finally shrugs his shoulders and goes to** DOMITILLA.

LURCIO   Domitilla . . .

DOMITILLA   ō Lurcio, trīstissima sum.

LURCIO **puts his arms around her, comforting her.**

LURCIO   Domitilla, ego tē amō, ego tē cūrō. nunc ego quoque sum lībertus.

DOMITILLA **stops crying and looks more cheerful.**

Domitilla, in culīnā adsunt pāvō et ostreae. ego tibi cēnam dō.

DOMITILLA   ō Lurcio, dēliciae meae!

LURCIO   et *ego* tē in mātrimōnium dūcō.

Exeunt.

| corculum | *sweetheart* | adsunt | *there are* |

A NOTE TO THE PRODUCER

The audience will need to believe in the master long before he is seen. Spend time discussing where he is when the slaves are talking about him, and how they behave when they know he is out. After all, their love for each other, if that is what it is, must be seen to be secret and risky. Then keep the pace going towards the end. Don't give the audience time to wonder whether they believe in the story!

PROPS

To provide, find, improvise or imagine.

DOMITILLA needs floor-washing equipment.
LURCIO has a bowl and a spoon to indicate his role as a
    cook. Later, he brings on a tray with at least two wine
    cups.
CONGRIO has a small flask (of poison)
MEGADORUS wears a toga ("dirty" he says), and is carrying
    a cloak which he gives to ANTHRAX.

PYRAMUS AND THISBE

INTRODUCTION

The story of Pyramus and Thisbe was well-known in Roman times. A picture of Pyramus, Thisbe and the lion decorated a wall in one of the biggest houses in Pompeii. A Roman poet, Ovid, told the story in full.

The version here is similar to the retelling by William Shakespeare. In *A Midsummer Night's Dream* Act V, Scene 1 he has a cast of working men acting out the story for their King and his lady. The simple efforts of Bottom the Weaver and his companions provide amusement for Theseus and Hippolyta as well as comedy for the audience.

CHARACTERS

NARRATOR
WALL
PYRAMUS
THISBE
LION
MOON (non-speaking)

The stage is empty. Enter NARRATOR. The other characters appear as each one is introduced by the NARRATOR.

NARRATOR   dominī et dominae, nōs vōbīs fābulam nārrāre volumus. hic vir est Pȳramus. haec fēmina pulcherrima est Thisbē. hic vir mūrus est. rīmam habet.

WALL **shows a crack between his fingers.**

dominī et dominae	*ladies and gentlemen*
volumus	*we want*
rīmam	*crack, chink*

saepe columbae per rīmam susurrant. haec fēmina lūna est,
quod nox est. nox est obscūra, sed vidēre possumus quod
lūna lūcet. fēmina igitur lanternam portat.

MOON **takes a position at the corner of the stage and stays there motionless throughout the play.**

hoc animal ferōx est leō. leō fremit. (*Lion roars.*) sed nūllum
est perīculum. ego nārrātor nunc discēdō. hī hominēs
fābulam vōbīs agere possunt.

The NARRATOR, PYRAMUS, THISBE **and** LION **leave.** WALL **and** MOON **remain.**

WALL   mē spectāte. ego sum mūrus. mūrus rīmam habet. vultisne
meam rīmam vidēre? vultisne per meam rīmam spectāre? per
hanc rīmam amātōrēs semper susurrābant.

Enter PYRAMUS.

PYRAMUS   obscūra nox! nox obscūra, nox obscūrissima! sed Thisbē
non adest. ō mūre, tū inter hortōs stās. ego volō rīmam
vidēre. per rīmam spectāre volō. (*He looks through the
crack.*) quis adest? nēmo adest. Thisbē nōn adest. Thisbēn
nōn videō. ō mūre, tē vituperō. pestis! furcifer!

Enter THISBE, **on the other side of the wall.**

THISBE   ō mūre, mūre, ubi est meus Pȳramus? eī ōsculum dare volō.

vidēre	*to see*	susurrābant	*used to whisper*
possumus	*we are able*	inter	*between*
lanternam	*lamp*	volō	*I want*
perīculum	*danger*	Thisbēn	*Thisbe* (accusative): a Greek
agere	*to act*		name with a Greek ending
possunt	*are able*	ubi?	*where?*
vultisne?	*do you want?*	eī	*to him*
spectāre	*to look*	ōsculum	*a kiss*
amātōrēs	*lovers*	dare	*to give*

PYRAMUS   vōcem videō. nunc meae Thisbēs vultum audīre volō.
ō Thisbē!

THISBE   ō suspīrium meum! ō Pȳrame! Pȳramus adest.

PYRAMUS   Thisbē adest. ō Thisbē! ōsculum tibi dare volō.

PYRAMUS tries but kisses only the wall; THISBE also only kisses the wall.

THISBE   ōsculum dō, sed mūrō ōsculum dō, nōn tibi.

PYRAMUS   cōnsilium capiō. prope amphitheātrum quam celerrimē
venī! ibi tē videō.

THISBE   ita vērō. prope amphitheātrum . . . quam celerrimē.

They hurry off in different directions. Enter the LION. He seems to have just made a meal of something very bloody. He wipes his messy, blood-stained mouth and speaks to the audience.

LION   ego vōs terrēre nōlō. ego nōn ferōx sum. cēnam iam
cōnsūmpsī. (*He wipes his lips again.*) sed fremere volō.

The LION gives a roar. Then THISBE enters, without noticing the LION.

THISBE   adsum. sed ubi est Pȳramus?

Suddenly THISBE notices the LION.

THISBE   ō!

As THISBE runs off, her cloak falls to the ground. The LION picks it up in his blood-stained mouth, toys with it and then lets it fall again. The LION exits. Enter PYRAMUS.

PYRAMUS   adsum. quam laetus sum. sed ubi est Thisbē? eam invenīre
nōn possum.

vōcem	*voice*	suspīrium	*heart-throb*
vōcem videō	*(the actor seems to*	terrēre	*to frighten*
	remember the scene in	nōlō	*I don't want*
	Shakespeare)	fremere	*to roar*
meae Thisbēs	*of my Thisbe*	invenīre	*to find*
vultum	*face*	possum	*I am able*
audīre	*to hear*		

He finds the cloak.

> ecce, lacerna! lacerna est sanguinolenta. ō hercle! minimē! minimē! ō leō, quid fēcistī? Thisbēn cōnsūmpsistī. Thisbē mortua est. ō dēliciae meae! ō mea columba! mortua es. vītam agere sine tē ego nōn possum.

He draws a sword and commits an extravagant suicide.

> nunc ego mortuus sum . . . mortuus . . . mortuissimus!

Enter THISBE.

THISBE   ō Pȳrame! Pȳrame! ubi es?

She finds him.

> num obdormīvistī? cūr iam dormīs? ēheu! mortuus est. mortuus es. ō dēliciae meae! ō mea columba! ego nōn possum sine tē vītam agere. mē quoque necō.

THISBE **too commits suicide. Enter** NARRATOR.

NARRATOR   ēheu! ita fābulam ēgērunt. placetne vōbīs? plaudīte!

lacerna	*cloak*	necō	*I kill*
sanguinolenta	*stained with blood*	fābulam ēgērunt	*have acted the play*
vītam agere	*to live*	placetne?	*does it please?*
num . . .	*you haven't, have you?*		

A NOTE TO THE PRODUCER

Some of the audience may have the Shakespeare scene in mind. So the actors have to be clear what they are doing—are they just telling a story, pretending to be Shakespearian, or acting at being actors? You might try simply being yourselves. If you go for a caricature, you will have to keep the play moving fast!

PROPS

To provide, find, improvise or imagine.

WALL   a costume: perhaps some plain rough curtain-
length material, painted to look like a brick surface.
A cardboard hat to look like a tile might be possible.

MOON   a lamp

THISBE   a cloak to drop

PYRAMUS   a sword

THE RATTLE

INTRODUCTION

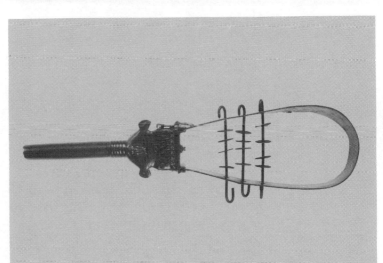

sīstrum *a rattle*

The *sistrum* in the picture was used in the religious ceremonies of the goddess Isis, to make a cheerful noise and drown out any unlucky sounds.

This play imagines two pupils exploring Pompeii on a school trip to Southern Italy. The town has great atmosphere. If you have a good imagination, the place can "come alive" for you even in bright sunlight. Anyone who was there alone, late at night, would be even more likely to be affected.

The play they see at the theatre seems to involve a handsome but silly young man who has fallen in love with a slave girl. There is a bad-tempered father to hinder them. This is the sort of comedy that Plautus translated from Greek into Latin for Roman audiences. His plays were popular entertainments, as were the *pantomimī* telling stories of legendary passion, through dance and mime. Tragedy did not please many Romans.

CHARACTERS

LUCY $\Big\}$ modern girls
JO

THREE HERALDS

SLAVE

SLAVE GIRL

THREE FARMERS

TWO CITIZENS

TWO YOUTHS

AEMILIUS

JULIA, wife of Aemilius

AEMILIA, daughter of Aemilius

TWO BOYS

MALE ACTOR   who plays "the slave"

FELIX   who plays "the drunken youth"

FEMALE ACTOR   who plays "the slave girl"

ACTIUS   who plays "the father"

The scene is the large theatre at Pompeii. The stage is in darkness. Two girls, LUCY and JO, enter with a torch and start looking for something.

LUCY   I didn't think Pompeii could feel so eerie! This is the theatre. Are you sure this is where you lost your watch?

JO   Yes, because when Mrs Hackford called us to go, I looked at the time, and then I jumped down the steps here . . .

LUCY   The theatre seats.

JO   And when we got back to the hotel in Naples it had gone.

LUCY   Look! There's something shining!

JO   Yes. That's my watch, but it's stuck in a crack. Help me lift this stone.

They pull up a large stone.

LUCY   Look! What's that?

JO **holds up a rattle.**

> JO It's some kind of rattle or something . . .

She shakes it. At once a flute starts playing, and ghosts start to glide in.

> LUCY Help! Someone's coming. Hide! Quick!

The GIRLS **move away and hide. Lights come on, and the ghosts become "alive."**
Trumpets sound. THREE HERALDS **enter.**

> HERALD I āctōrēs adsunt.
>
> HERALD 2 Sorex et Actius adsunt.
>
> HERALD 3 Gaius Aemilius Secundus in theātrō fābulam dat.
>
> HERALD I contendite ad theātrum. Aemilius fābulam optimam dat.

The HERALDS **stand aside. A** SLAVE **and a** SLAVE GIRL **enter, and take their places in**
the stage audience.

> SLAVE habēsne cibum?
>
> SLAVE GIRL ita vērō. cibum habeō. āctōrēs mihi placent. Sorex est
> suspīrium meum!

THREE FARMERS **enter.**

> FARMER I euge! hodie nos agricolae nōn labōrāmus!
>
> FARMER 2 quis est Aemilius Secundus?
>
> FARMER 3 est argentārius dīves.

The FARMERS **take their places in the audience. Two** CITIZENS **enter.**

> CITIZEN I pantomīmus mihi placet. placetne tibi?
>
> CITIZEN 2 minimē. tragoedia mē dēlectat.

The CITIZENS **take their places.** TWO YOUTHS **enter.**

> YOUTH I contende!
>
> YOUTH 2 ego contendō, sed sunt in viā multī virī et multae fēminae.

suspīrium	*heart-throb*	tragoedia	*tragedy*
pantomīmus	*a mime actor*		

The YOUTHS **take their places.** AEMILIUS, **the sponsor, enters with** JULIA, **his wife, who is carrying a baby in her arms.** AEMILIA, **his daughter, is with them. They take the "best seats."**

SLAVE   ecce! Aemilius venit.

SLAVE GIRL   uxor et fīlia quoque veniunt. uxor parvum fīlium portat.

AEMILIUS, JULIA **and** AEMILIA **wave to the crowd.** TWO BOYS **enter.**

BOY 1   estne cavea plēna?

BOY 2   minimē. ecce! est locus in summā caveā. locum cōnspiciō.

The BOYS **take their places, at the back. The** MALE ACTOR **enters and whispers something to** AEMILIUS. AEMILIUS **stands up.**

AEMILIUS   tacēte! tacēte! tacēte, omnēs! hodiē Sorex aeger est.

Groans from the crowd.

Fēlīx, igitur, optimus āctor, hodiē fābulam agit.

The crowd shouts in approval. "euge!" "bene!" Then the play begins. The MALE ACTOR, **as a slave, enters wearing a grotesque mask.** AEMILIUS' **baby cries, and his wife,** JULIA, **shakes the rattle to quieten it.**

JULIA   tacē! tacē, dulcissime!

MALE ACTOR   ego servus sum. Mārcus, dominus meus, est iuvenis. pulcher iuvenis est, sed stultus. iuvenis ancillam amat, sed ancilla patrī non placet.

FELIX, **as the drunken youth "Marcus" enters, with the** FEMALE ACTOR **as the "slave girl."**

FELIX   mea columba! meae dēliciae! ego tē amō!

ACTIUS, **as the "father," enters.**

ACTIUS   quid facis, Mārce? ēbriusne es?

---

in summā caveā	*in the topmost part of the seating area*	pulcher	*good-looking*
		patrī	*his father*
dulcissime	*(my) sweetest*		

A rumbling noise is heard.

AEMILIA	pater! ego tremōrēs sentiō.
JULIA	ego sonōs audiō.
AEMILIA	perterrita sum.
AEMILIUS	nōn sum sollicitus. iamprīdem terra tremuit, sed larēs nōs servāvērunt. (*speaking to the actors*) fābulam agite!

There is more rumbling.

SLAVE GIRL	iterum terra tremuit.
ACTIUS	(*as himself*) ecce! mōns!
FELIX	(*as himself*) ego nūbem mīrābilem videō.
MALE ACTOR	(*as himself*) ego flammās videō.
FEMALE ACTOR	(*as herself*) mōns īrātissimus est.
AEMILIUS	tacēte! tacēte, omnēs! iamprīdem deī nōs servāvērunt. hodiē quoque nōs servant.
FARMER 1	ego tibi nōn crēdō. maiōrēs tremōrēs sentiō.
FARMER 2	ego cinerem sentiō.
FARMER 3	ego ad portum contendō. nāvem petō.

Exeunt the FARMERS.

CITIZEN 1	ego ad vīllam festīnō. rēs pretiōsās servāre volō.
CITIZEN 2	stultissimus es. ego portum petō.

Exeunt the CITIZENS.

BOY 1	curre ē theātrō!
BOY 2	festīnā!

Exeunt the BOYS.

AEMILIA	pater! venī! perīculōsum est.

servāre	*to save*	volō	*I want*

AEMILIUS   minimē, fīlia. larēs nōs cūrant.

There are more loud noises.

   ACTIUS   (*as himself*) nōs fābulam nōn agimus.

   FELIX   (*as himself*) ad portum fugimus.

AEMILIA   ego vōbīscum veniō.

The ACTORS leave the stage and flee. AEMILIA follows them. AEMILIUS shouts after them.

AEMILIUS   manēte! quō festīnātis? Aemilia, venī ad mē!

There is a loud crash. JULIA drops the rattle. All the Pompeians run off in various directions. The lights go out. The GIRLS come forward, wide-eyed.

   JO   So that's where the rattle came from. (*She tries to understand what has been happening.*) They'll never believe us.

   LUCY   Let's go back to the hotel. What's the time? Your watch . . . ? Is it still going?

   JO   Yes, it's two minutes to midnight, *and* it's August 24th.

      vōbīscum   *with you*

A NOTE TO THE PRODUCER

Your task must be to make a dream come true. If you have control over lighting, that will help. If not, your actors have got to be able to "freeze" so that they let each other have the audience's attention.

The other problem will be that in Pompeii you have actors who start off playing parts in a play and then come out of it. Probably the most important thing is to create a sense of *where* everything happens—not just "in the theatre," but precisely where on stage, and precisely where in the auditorium. Make sure all your actors know where Mount Vesuvius is!

PROPS

To provide, find, improvise or imagine.

Sound effects are needed. They can perhaps be provided electronically through a recording device, or perhaps by banging on a tin tray.

The lost watch needs to be planted on stage, with a rattle placed nearby.

The GIRLS carry a torch.

The SLAVE GIRL has food with her.

JULIA has a "baby"; she also has a rattle when she comes on: it may need two rattles or a slick exchange when the GIRLS move away and hide.

The four ACTORS could use and wear masks, and take them off when they run away.

SACRIFICE

INTRODUCTION

The priest at a Roman religious ceremony was usually a citizen distinguished through his wealth or political position. He had no particular religious training and might not even have any religious feelings. At a sacrifice, when a victim was offered to the gods, the priest was helped by specialist attendants, who brought forward the animal, carried out the killing, dealt with the blood and advised about any omens and signs that might be seen in the actions of the animal or in its dead body.

In this play, ANTONIUS has the duty of carrying out a sacrifice to the chief of the gods, Jupiter, at an altar in front of the god's statue. Both he and his family would rather be doing something else.

There were stories told of the gods punishing irreligious human beings and rewarding the few good people left on earth. You might like to compare Ovid's story of Deucalion (in *Metamorphoses*, Book I) with the Bible-story of Noah, in *Genesis* chapters 6–8.

CHARACTERS

TWO ATTENDANTS at sacrifice
ANTONIUS, priest
CLAUDIA, his wife
MARCUS
CORNELIA } their children
TULLIA
OLD MAN, father of Antōnius
OLD WOMAN, mother of Antōnius
LEADING ACTOR, and other ACTORS
ACROBATS
JUGGLERS
MUSICIANS

STATUE OF JUPITER (becomes Jupiter)
STATUE OF MERCURY
STATUE OF APOLLO
CITIZENS (up to ten; assign the parts accordingly)

**The scene is outside a temple in Pompeii. An altar is at the centre of the stage.
THREE STATUES stand on pedestals. TWO ATTENDANTS enter and check that the
altar is ready for the sacrifice.**

ATTENDANT 1   omnia sunt parāta.

ATTENDANT 2   sacrificia semper deīs placent.

ATTENDANT 1   ita vērō.

ATTENDANT 1 **points to the** STATUE OF JUPITER.

quam splendidus est hic Iūppiter noster.

The ATTENDANTS **go out. The** STATUE OF JUPITER **turns to the other** STATUES.

STATUE OF
JUPITER   hodiē est sacrificium mīrābile.

STATUE OF
MERCURY   euge! placetne tibi?

STATUE OF
JUPITER   ita vērō, mihi maximē placet. ego sum optimus et maximus.

The STATUES **"freeze" again. The family enters: the** OLD MAN, **the** OLD WOMAN,
ANTONIUS, CLAUDIA, MARCUS, CORNELIA **and** TULLIA, **followed at a distance by**
CITIZENS, **and** TWO ATTENDANTS, **one bringing the victim.**

MARCUS   (*with childish curiosity*) cūr tū haec vestīmenta splendida
geris, pater?

OLD WOMAN   pater tuus est sacerdōs, Mārce. hodiē prō templō civēs

---

Iūppiter	*Jupiter, Jove* (the more usual Roman spelling	vestīmenta	*clothes*
		sacerdōs	*priest*
maximē	*very much*	prō templō	*in front of the temple*
haec	*these*		

sacrificium Iovī et aliīs deīs faciunt. pater tuus, ut sacerdōs, hoc sacrificium facit.

MARCUS   (*sulkily*) nōlō ad sacrificium īre.

CORNELIA   (*also sulkily*) volō hīc cum frātre manēre.

TULLIA   (*also sulkily*) ego nōlō sacrificium vidēre.

ANTONIUS confesses his true feelings.

ANTONIUS   neque ego volō sacrificium facere. nōn mē dēlectat. magis mihi placent thermae.

OLD MAN   (*indignantly*) tacē, Antōnī! necesse est nōbīs hoc sacrificium facere quod Iūppiter semper nōs adiuvat, semper nōs servat. necesse est nōbīs Iovī dōna dare. necesse est nōbīs Iovī grātiās agere.

ANTONIUS   (*giving in*) ita vērō, pater, ita vērō.

OLD WOMAN   sumus omnēs parātī?

CLAUDIA   parātī sumus.

ANTONIUS   festīnāte, ō cīvēs! ad sacrificium venīmus.

The CITIZENS gather with the FAMILY around the altar.

CITIZEN 1   quam pulchra est haec victima.

CITIZEN 2   sacrificium splendidum hodiē faciunt.

ANTONIUS   nunc sacrificium facimus.

He rearranges his toga to cover his head.

(*in a formal voice*) silentium poscō. tacēte omnēs.

Iovī	*to Jupiter*		facere	*to make*
ut	*as*		magis	*more*
nōlō	*I don't want*		necesse est	*it is necessary*
īre	*to go*		nōbīs	*for us*
volō	*I want*		dare	*to give*
hīc	*here*		grātiās agere	*to give thanks*
manēre	*to stay*		victima	*a victim for sacrifice*
vidēre	*to see*		silentium poscō	*I call for silence*
neque ego	*nor do I*			

ANTONIUS **sprinkles flour on to the victim's head. Then he gives the order to** ATTENDANT 2.

victimam necā!

ATTENDANT 2   parātus sum.

But just as he is about to cut the animal's throat, in come various ACTORS, ACROBATS, JUGGLERS **and** MUSICIANS. **The** CHILDREN **are delighted.**

MARCUS   euge! āctōrēs adsunt.

CLAUDIA   tacē! sacrificium spectā!

LEADING   ecce! āctōrēs adsumus. (*to Marcus*) vīsne āctōrēs vidēre?
ACTOR   sunt optimī. (*to all the children*) venīte mēcum.

MARCUS   venīmus.

The LEADING ACTOR **leads the** CHILDREN **away from the altar to another part of the stage.**

LEADING
ACTOR   venīte, puerī! puellae, venīte!

The ADULTS **also turn and slowly follow the** CHILDREN. **Even** ATTENDANT 1 **follows. They surround the performing** ACTORS **and "freeze." Only the** OLD MAN, OLD WOMAN **and** ATTENDANT 2, **who are obviously upset, remain near the altar.**

OLD MAN   ō deī immortālēs! ō Iūppiter! revenīte, cīvēs! sacrificium
facimus.

STATUE OF
JUPITER   revenīte, cīvēs, ad sacrificium.

ATTENDANT 2 **is still preparing to kill the victim, but he is distracted, and the victim exits, bleating "baaa . . . baaa".** ATTENDANT 2 **pursues it. The** STATUE OF JUPITER **makes thunder noises. The** OLD MAN **and** OLD WOMAN **are terrified.**

OLD MAN   ō mē miserum! quid facere possumus?

OLD WOMAN   malum! horribile! rem malam, rem horribilem exspectāmus.

vīsne?	*do you want?*	quid facere possumus?	*what can we do?*
immortālēs	*immortal*	malum	*evil*
miserum	*wretched*	horribile	*dreadful*

OLD MAN   ēheu! ō mē miserum! ō Iūppiter, tē ōrāmus, quod tū es
                optimus et maximus . . .

Sounds from Mount Vesuvius are heard in the distance. The sacrifice scene "freezes." Around the ACTORS the CROWD comes to life.

CITIZEN 1   audīsne sonōs?

CITIZEN 2   minimē. āctōrēs spectā!

The OLD MAN turns from the sacrifice and pleads.

OLD MAN   revenīte, ō cīvēs!

But the ACTORS, ACROBATS, JUGGLERS and MUSICIANS go on performing.

CITIZENS   (*variously*) saltant! . . . saliunt! . . . ecce, pilās iactant! . . .
                quam callidī sunt!

The CROWD's entertainment "freezes." At the other part of the stage, the STATUE OF JUPITER makes louder thunder noises.

OLD MAN   ō Iūppiter, veniam petimus. sunt ignāvī et stultissimī illī
                cīvēs.

OLD WOMAN   veniam petimus, ō maxime Iūppiter.

STATUE OF
JUPITER   (*loudly*) ego īrātissimus sum, īrātissimus.

He points towards the mountain.

                mōns Vesuvī, dēlē omnem hunc populum. dēlē omnem
                urbem. dēlē omnia.

There is a moment of silence, then louder thunder noises. All the humans are terrified.

CITIZENS   (*variously*) quid audīvistī? . . . sonōs audiō . . . quam
                perterritus sum! . . . ecce, terra tremit! . . . fortasse īrātī
                sunt deī . . . ita vērō, victima effūgit . . . deī immortālēs,
                quid facere possumus? . . . effuge, effuge! . . . terra tremit
                . . . fugite, amīcī, fugite!

ōrāmus	*we beseech*	veniam	*favour*
saltant	*dance*	populum	*nation, people*
pilās iactant	*they juggle balls*	omnia	*everything*

In panic, the CROWD flees. The OLD MAN and OLD WOMAN are left, still standing beside the altar.

OLD MAN   servā nōs, ō Iūppiter! nōs sumus iūstī. semper tē adōrāmus.

STATUE OF   vērum dīcis. vōs semper mē dēlectāvistis. Mercurī, hūc venī!
JUPITER   Apollo, hūc venī!

The other STATUES descend from their pedestals.

     dūcite hunc senem et uxōrem ad Olympum montem. eōs servāmus quod semper iūstī erant. (*to the old couple*) vōs immortālēs estis et fēlīcēs inter nōs in Olympō monte.

OLD WOMAN   tibi grātiās agimus, ō Iūppiter.

The OLD MAN, OLD WOMAN and the gods JUPITER, MERCURY and APOLLO look back to where the townspeople were.

OLD MAN   ō miserōs Pompēiōs! o miseram urbem!

OLD WOMAN   ō miserōs Pompēiānōs!

iūstī	*just*	inter	*among*
adōrāmus	*we worship*	miserōs	*wretched*
vērum	*truth*	Pompēiōs	*Pompeii*
hunc	*this*		

A NOTE TO THE PRODUCER

The success of this play will depend on the ability of the actors to "freeze"—to remain totally still when not "acting." The statues must freeze before coming to life as Jupiter and his fellow gods, and the altar scene can be visible at the same time as the other preparations, so long as the actors freeze and allow the audience to concentrate entirely on what is going on elsewhere.

It will be a challenge to create a satisfactory victim. It is quiet (stunned, drugged?) until the moment of escape, but then has to get off-stage fast. Perhaps the audience won't notice some strong black thread!

PROPS

To provide, find, improvise or imagine.

Sound effects are needed. They can perhaps be provided electronically through a recording device, or perhaps by banging a tin tray.

A dusting of powder may help the gods look like marble statues.

At the altar, you will need: a victim, a knife, flour.

You will also need equipment for the entertainers.

LITTLE RED RIDING HOOD

INTRODUCTION

To make a Latin play about a well-known story demands some unfamiliar vocabulary. Here *purpureus* is the adjective which the Romans used for a bright and impressive colour which we might call purple or red. (Romans were not very good at distinguishing colours.) *paenula* is a combined cloak and hood, a thick blanket-like wrap which also protected the head.

It is unusual to call someone by the name of a piece of clothing, but the emperor Gaius was called Caligula, after *caliga*, the name for a Roman soldier's boot. This came about because Gaius was brought up in a Roman camp where his father was commander. The little boy had a little soldier outfit, with little boots to fit. He was much cherished by the ordinary soldiers, and some might think he was spoiled by them!

CHARACTERS

MOTHER of Poppaea
POPPAEA
WOLF
TWO HUNTERS
GRANDMOTHER

The scene is a kitchen. Poppaea's MOTHER is packing a basket.

MOTHER   ēheu! valdē sollicitus sum, quod māter mea est aegra. in mediā silvā habitat sōla. cibum et vīnum ad eam mittō. ubi est fīlia mea? Poppaea! Poppaea!

ubi?   *where?*

Enter POPPAEA.

POPPAEA   quid est, māter?

MOTHER   Poppaea, necesse est tibi aviam tuam vīsitāre, quod aegra est. ecce! cibum et vīnum parāvī. age igitur, parvam paenulam purpuream indue!

MOTHER **holds out the little red cloak for** POPPAEA **to put on, and then hands her the basket.**

       fer cibum et vīnum et nunc per silvam ad aviam contende.

POPPAEA   valē, māter!

MOTHER   valē, Poppaea!

POPPAEA **exits. The lights go down and** MOTHER **exits. The scene now changes to a dark wood. Enter** POPPAEA.

POPPAEA   quam fessa sum! iter longum est ad vīllam ubi avia mea habitat. necesse est mihi sedēre.

POPPAEA **sits down. The** WOLF **enters unseen, and addresses the audience.**

WOLF   ō mē miserum! est lupīs nūlla pāx data. vēnātōrēs iterum adsunt in silvā. vēnātōrēs mihi nōn placent.

The WOLF **sees** POPPAEA.

       sed quid videō? parvam puellam videō. puellae mihi valdē placent. hanc puellam cōnsūmere volō. nunc tamen puellam cōnsūmere nōn possum, quod vēnātōrēs prope sunt. sed spectāte! nam callidus sum. (*to Poppaea*) salvē, puella! tū fessa es?

necesse est	*it is necessary*	sedēre	*to sit down*
tibi	*for you*	miserum	*wretched*
aviam	*grandmother*	data	*given*
vīsitāre	*to visit*	cōnsūmere	*to eat*
age!	*come on!*	volō	*I want*
fer!	*carry! take!*	possum	*I am able*
fessa	*tired*	prope	*nearby*
mihi	*for me*	nam	*for*

POPPAEA   ita vērō. longum iter faciō.

WOLF   quō ambulās?

POPPAEA   ad vīllam ubi avia mea habitat ambulō. cibum et vīnum ferō, quod aegra est avia mea.

WOLF   ubi habitat avia tua?

POPPAEA   (*pointing*) in mediā silvā habitat, prope fontem.

The WOLF **turns to the audience with a knowing look.**

WOLF   aa! (*to Poppaea*) festīnā lentē, mea columba. fortasse tē iterum videō. valē!

POPPAEA   valē!

Exit WOLF, **purposefully.**

quam benignus erat iste lupus.

POPPAEA **continues on her way slowly.**

ecce! quam pulchrī sunt flōrēs!

POPPAEA **stops to gather flowers. Enter** TWO HUNTERS.

HUNTER 1   salvē, Parva Paenula Purpurea!

POPPAEA   salvēte, amīcī!

HUNTER 2   quō ambulās?

POPPAEA   ad vīllam ubi avia mea habitat ambulō. cibum et vīnum ferō, quod aegra est avia mea. et vōs, quid facitis?

HUNTER 1   nos agitāmus lupum quī per silvam currit. cautē igitur prōcēde, Parva Paenula Purpurea. valē!

POPPAEA   valēte!

Exeunt.

fontem	*a spring*	flōrēs	*flowers*
lentē	*slowly* ("hurry slowly" is good advice; sometimes = "more haste, less speed.")	quī	*which*

The scene changes to the GRANDMOTHER's house. GRANDMOTHER is in bed. The WOLF approaches the door and knocks.

GRANDMOTHER   quis iānuam pulsat?

WOLF   (*in a young girl's voice*) ego Poppaea, neptis tua, iānuam pulsō.

GRANDMOTHER   intrā, Poppaea!

The WOLF enters, eats up the GRANDMOTHER, then shuts the door and gets into bed. Now POPPAEA appears and knocks.

WOLF   (*imitating Grandmother's weak voice*) quis iānuam pulsat?

POPPAEA   (*to herself*) babae! certē avia mea moribunda est. (*aloud*) ego Popaea, neptis tua, iānuam pulsō.

WOLF   intrā, Poppaea!

He pulls up the bedclothes and chuckles.

venī hūc, Poppaea! sedē prope mē!

POPPAEA comes near, and sits looking wide-eyed at the disguised WOLF.

POPPAEA   ō avia mea, quantās aurēs habēs!

WOLF   melius igitur tē audiō, Poppaea.

POPPAEA   ō avia mea, quantōs oculōs habēs!

WOLF   melius igitur tē videō, Poppaea.

POPPAEA   ō avia mea, quantōs dentēs habēs!

WOLF   melius igitur tē cōnsūmō, Poppaea.

The WOLF leaps out of bed. POPPAEA screams. At this moment the TWO HUNTERS enter.

HUNTER I   pestis!

neptis	*granddaughter*	melius	*better*
quantās!	*what big!*	oculōs	*eyes*
aurēs	*ears*	dentēs	*teeth*

He kills the WOLF.

> HUNTER 2　lupus est mortuus, et tū, Parva Paenula Purpurea, es tūta.

A NOTE TO THE PRODUCER

Once you have got a good wolf mask, you are nearly
there. No one will mind if the wolf doesn't look or move
like a wolf, but make sure that he or she really acts up!

PROPS

To provide, find, improvise or imagine.

The red cloak for POPPAEA.
Basket
Goodies
Weapons for the HUNTERS to show their role, and later to
　　kill the wolf.
GRANDMOTHER's bed will be important: when she has been
　　"eaten" she will have to hide somewhere in the
　　bedclothes until the end.

THE DETECTIVE GAME

It is possible to make up a play *ex tempore* (the Latin words mean "on the spot"). The first act consists of a murder. Decide on the murderer, the place and the murder weapon. The murder can then be carried out before the audience.

The second act shows the solving of the mystery. There is a detective, called *inquīsītor*, and a list of characters:

domina pāvō	*virgō coccina*
lēgātus fulvus	*domina alba*
doctor cerasinus	*sacerdōs viridis*

and a list of locations:

in peristȳliō	*in latrīnā*
in ātriō	*in triclīniō*
in tablīnō	*in bibliothēcā*
in vestibulō	

A maid *ancilla* goes to get each character in turn. The detective says: "*dūc eum* OR *eam* OR (character's name—accusative) *ad mē.*" The maid says to each one: "*venī mēcum.*" The maid can also be used later to reveal untruths.

The detective asks: "*quis es tū?*" Each character answers: "*ego sum . . .*" The detective asks "*ubi erās tū?*" Each character answers: "*ego eram in . . .*" The detective may also ask about someone else: "*ubi erat X?*" The character being cross-examined may answer: "*X erat in . . . ,*" or may answer: "*nesciō.*"

lēgātus	*a military officer of high rank*	alba	*white*
fulvus	*yellow* (the colour of lions, and sand)	sacerdōs	*priest*
		viridis	*green*
cerasinus	*cherry like*	ubi?	*where?*
coccina	*scarlet*	nesciō	*I don't know*

If the maid is required to help solve the mystery, she contradicts a character as follows: "*minimē! ego eum* OR *eam* OR (character's name—accusative) *in . . . vīdī.*" When a character confesses, the words are: "*ego eum* OR *eam* OR (victim's name—accusative) *necāvī.*"

The full version of *The Detective Game* requires a list of weapons with which the murder might be committed:

rudente	*fūste plumbeō*
secūrī	*gladiō*
candēlābrō	*baculō*
sagittā	

You may need a board in the form of a Roman *domus*, rather than a stage.

---

rudente	*with a rope*		sagittā	*with an arrow*
secūrī	*with an axe*		plumbeō	*made of lead*
candēlābrō	*with a lampstand*		baculō	*with a stick*

VESUVIUS

INTRODUCTION

This is the toughest of the plays to perform. It shows a scene of everyday life in a small Italian town. It ends with the frightening signs of an earthquake and a volcanic eruption. The town is Pompeii in 79 A.D.

A teacher is introducing his pupils to some lines from the famous poet, Virgil. The lines describe preparations for a heroic boxing match. At outdoor schools the learning was done mostly by repetition and chanting. According to Martial, the noise could wake the neighbours early in the morning. Two drunks get involved in a quarrel. The Roman satire-writer, Juvenal, explained how hard it was to walk safely through the streets on a dark night. The signwriters come from Pompeii itself. In Pompeii, Aemilius wrote election slogans and signed his name. Florus and Fruttus are also mentioned on Pompeian walls. Whether their names are serious or "jokey" is not clear. M. Cerrinius Vatia was a genuine Pompeian candidate.

There is no evidence for Christians in Pompeii, and in fact 79 A.D. may be too early for Christianity to have reached a very small town in Southern Italy. Nevertheless, there were Christians in the Roman Empire at this time (St. Paul had reached Rome long before), and Pliny saw them as a problem in Bithynia only thirty or so years later.

What was it really like to be involved in the eruption of Vesuvius? Appendix I, p 71, provides three accounts. Two are letters by Pliny, who was staying nearby at the time. In them he describes the experience to a friend. He survived because he preferred to work at his school-Latin rather than to go into the danger area. The third account is of a later eruption and is from a report printed by *The Times* of London, 17th November 1868. Compare also the picture on page 73.

CHARACTERS

TWO DRUNKS
SLAVES 1 & 2, attending the second drunk
AEMILIUS
FLORUS } signwriters
FRUTTUS
MERCHANT (non-speaking)
BREADSELLER
MARCUS } Christians
PHILIPPUS
LUCIUS, a good pupil
SLAVE 3, Lūcius' paedagogus
TEACHER
PUBLIUS, a late pupil
SLAVE 4, Pūblius' paedagogus
DECIMUS, a bad pupil
SLAVES 5 & 6, attending on Decimus
NEIGHBOUR

The scene is a street in Pompeii. DRUNK 1 is discovered lying mid-stage. Enter three signwriters in a line: FLORUS **carrying lamp and paint**, AEMILIUS **carrying a short ladder horizontally on his shoulder, and** FRUTTUS **carrying a bucket. It is dark, and they are creeping in quietly so as not to be noticed.** FLORUS **turns to whisper to** AEMILIUS.

> FLORUS   stt! tacē!

AEMILIUS **turns to pass the message on to** FRUTTUS.

> AEMILIUS   tacē!

FRUTTUS **too turns to pass the message on.**

> FRUTTUS   tacē!

Of course, there is no one behind him. Puzzled, AEMILIUS **looks right round to see, and the ladder strikes** FRUTTUS.

AEMILIUS   quō prōcēdimus? quid quaeris, lanternārī?

FLORUS   mūrum quaerō.

FRUTTUS **hasn't heard properly.**

FRUTTUS   quid quaerit?

FLORUS **and** AEMILIUS **both turn to tell him; the ladder strikes** FRUTTUS **again!**

AEMILIUS   mūrum.

FRUTTUS   ah!

AEMILIUS   habēsne titulum?

FLORUS   ecce! hīc habeō.

FRUTTUS   quid habēs?

FLORUS **and** AEMILIUS **again turn round; the ladder strikes** FRUTTUS **a third time.**

FLORUS ⎱
          ⎰ (*loudly*) titulum!
AEMILIUS

AEMILIUS   quid est?

FLORUS   (*sarcastically*) quid est?

FRUTTUS   (*rather loudly*) quid est?

FLORUS ⎱
          ⎰ tacē!
AEMILIUS

FLORUS **and** AEMILIUS **stop suddenly, so that** FRUTTUS **walks into them. He is careful not to spill what is in his bucket.** AEMILIUS **puts down the ladder.** FLORUS **holds up the lamp.** FLORUS **starts to read from a scrap of papyrus.**

FLORUS   "Mārcum Cerrinium Vatiam rogāmus."

AEMILIUS **reads over** FLORUS' **shoulder, and plans the exact wording.**

AEMILIUS   "Mārcum Cerrinium Vatiam . . . scrīpsit Aemilius. aderant
             Flōrus et Fruttus."

lanternārī	*lamp-carrier*	rogāmus	*ask support for*
hīc	*here*		

FLORUS   minimē. "scrīpsit Flōrus, aderat Aemilius."

FRUTTUS   et Fruttus.

AEMILIUS   scrīpsit Aemilius. Flōrus aderat lanternārius.

FLORUS   scrīpsit Flōrus. Aemilius aderat et scālās portābat.

FRUTTUS   Fruttus quoque aderat.

A heavily laden MERCHANT goes by. The SIGNWRITERS stand still to avoid being noticed.

FLORUS ⎫
         ⎬ tacē!
AEMILIUS ⎭

When the MERCHANT has gone . . .

AEMILIUS   ego sum scrīptor. ego scrībō.

FLORUS   tūne scrībis? minimē. ego optimē scrībō.

FRUTTUS moves towards the wall with his bucket.

FRUTTUS   ego sum dealbātor. hic est mūrus. est mūrus pulcher.

He whitewashes it.

ecce! iam mūrum fēcī pulchriōrem.

A BREADSELLER enters. He chants as in a traditional "street cry."

BREADSELLER   pānem, eme pānem!

The SIGNWRITERS ignore him.

FLORUS   mūrum pulchriōrem numquam vīdī.

AEMILIUS   est mūrus pulcherrimus. dā mihi!

He grabs the paint pot from FLORUS.

tenē scālās . . .

BREADSELLER   (*still chanting*) pānem, eme pānem!

scālās   *ladder*
dealbātor   *whitener, the man who creates a white background for a*
                 slogan.

The BREADSELLER **exits. The** SIGNWRITERS **continue to quarrel among themselves. Enter** DRUNK 2, **supported by** SLAVES 1 & 2.

DRUNK 2	serve, fer . . .
SLAVE 1	quid?
DRUNK 2	fer . . . fer . . .
SLAVE 2	num ēbrius est?
SLAVE 1	ita vērō, ēbrius, iterum ēbrius, semper ēbrius.
DRUNK 2	fer . . .
SLAVE 1	fer dominum.
DRUNK 2	lūna mē domum dūcit.
SLAVE 2	sed lūna nōn lūcet.

DRUNK 1 **gets up unsteadily from his position in mid-stage, and is looking for a fight. The** SLAVES **keep a low profile and leave the** TWO DRUNKS **staggering at each other.**

DRUNK 1	unde venīs? nīl mihi respondēs? aut dīc aut accipe . . .

DRUNK 1 **lashes out and hits** DRUNK 2.

SLAVE 2	rixa est.
DRUNK 1	ubi tē quaerō, furcifer?

The TWO DRUNKS **grapple clumsily. Then they fall apart, and apparently fall asleep.**

SLAVE 1	ecce! somnum rixa facit.

Enter MARCUS **secretively. The others remain still in the background.**

MARCUS	nōx est. lūna tamen nōn lūcet. ego ē vīllā discēdō, sed perterritus sum. sum servus. ego Chrīstō crēdō.

fer!	*bring! carry!*	rixa	*brawl*
num?	*he isn't, is he?*	ubi?	*where?*
domum	*home*	somnum	*sleep*
unde?	*where from?*	facit	*causes*
nīl = nihil	*nothing*	Chrīstō	*Christ*
aut . . . aut	*either . . . or*		

He makes a Christian sign.

>   ego sum Chrīstiānus.

Enter PHILIPPUS **also secretively.**

PHILIPPUS   (*whispering*) Mārce.

MARCUS   quis est?

PHILIPPUS   ego, Philippus. esne parātus?

MARCUS   sum parātus, sed perterritus sum.

PHILIPPUS   crēde deō. ego quoque sum servus. sed nōs Chrīstiānī sumus. nōs Chrīstō crēdimus.

MARCUS   quō prōcēdimus?

PHILIPPUS   prōcēdimus ad frātrēs. omnēs cibum capimus. omnēs cantāmus. tum discēdimus et ante lūcem ad dominōs revenīmus. crēde deō, mī frāter!

They move quietly off. Enter LUCIUS, **a good pupil, striding eagerly to school, followed by** SLAVE 3, **Lucius' paedagogus, who is carrying all the school equipment.**

LUCIUS   ecce, adsum. portāsne stilum?

SLAVE 3   ecce, stilus.

LUCIUS   portāsne cērās?

SLAVE 3   ecce, cērae.

LUCIUS   portāsne tabulās?

SLAVE 3   ecce, omnia habeō. optimus sum capsārius.

LUCIUS   quid herī fēcimus? . . . Vergilius . . . liber quīntus.

He begins to recite Virgil word for word and continues quietly, during the following action, for as long as he can remember. (See Appendix II.)

ante	*before*
mi	*my (dear)*
tabulās	*wooden tablets* (perhaps a better quality than cerae)
capsārius	*book-box carrier*
quīntus	*fifth*

LUCIUS   haec fātus duplicem . . . (*etc.*)

By now, AEMILIUS is on the ladder and writing.

AEMILIUS   V–a–t–i–a–m . . . quis rogat?

FLORUS   nōs scrīptōrēs rogāmus.

AEMILIUS   minimē . . .

FRUTTUS   ego nōn rogō.

AEMILIUS   tacē! (*slowly*) rogant vīcīnī.

LUCIUS, **in his recitation, raises his voice.** AEMILIUS **hears him and turning on his ladder wobbles. The lantern wobbles.**

AEMILIUS   tenē, tenē!

The TEACHER enters.

TEACHER   (*to Lucius*) salvē!

LUCIUS **stops reciting for a moment.**

LUCIUS   salvē, magister!

TEACHER   (*to Slave 3*) discēde, paedagōge! sedē puer! sōlusne ades? ubi sunt aliī?

SLAVE 3 **goes back to a dark corner. Enter PUBLIUS, late as usual, followed at a run by SLAVE 4, his paedagogus. Both are still finishing their breakfasts.**

SLAVE 4   (*to audience*) ō calamitātem!

PUBLIUS   iam adsum, magister. festīnāvī. quam celerrimē festīnāvī.

TEACHER   (*quoting learnedly to himself*) sed sī tantus amor . . . incipiam. (*to slave 4*) discēde, paedagōge! sedē puer! quid herī lēgimus? a! . . . Pūblius Vergilius Maro . . . dē āthlētīs . . . dē pugilibus! quid est āthlēta?

LUCIUS   āthlēta currit.

haec	*these things*	calamitātem	*calamity, disaster*
fātus	*having spoken*	sī tantus amor	*if (your) desire (is) so*
duplicem	*double*		*great (the master is*
vīcīnī	*neighbours*		*quoting Virgil)*
magister	*schoolmaster*		

PUBLIUS ego quoque cucurrī.

TEACHER quid est pugil?

LUCIUS pugil pugnat.

PUBLIUS is jealous of LUCIUS and thumps him.

PUBLIUS ego quoque pugnō.

SLAVES 3 & 4 try to intervene, muttering.

SLAVE 3 ēheu, puerī pugnant.

There is a din, the TEACHER waves his stick, etc. The TEACHER begins reciting, to settle the uproar.

TEACHER haec fātus . . .

Enter DECIMUS, a bad pupil, dragged by SLAVES 5 & 6.

SLAVE 5 (*coaxingly*) venī, domine parve, venī ad lūdum.

DECIMUS minimē, mihi nōn placet.

SLAVE 5 sed dominus, pater tuus, tē iussit. domina, māter tua, tē iussit.

DECIMUS mihi nōn placet. lūdus mē nōn dēlectat. magister mē nōn dēlectat.

DECIMUS deliberately drops something he is carrying. As SLAVE 5 stoops to pick it up, DECIMUS kicks him.

SLAVE 6 (*twisting Decimus' arm*) ego tē adiuvō.

Meanwhile, the TEACHER's voice has been swamped by this noise. He summons DECIMUS.

TEACHER ecce, tertius discipulus. venī, venī celerrimē!

SLAVES 5 & 6 join the other SLAVES in the corner.

TEACHER nōs dē pugilibus dīcimus.

incipiam	*I will begin*	discipulus	*pupil*
lūdum	*school*	celerrimē	*very quickly*
iussit	*gave orders*		

The CLASS of three all join in the recitation, from the beginning. The TEACHER interrupts to ask questions.

> CLASS   haec fātus . . .
>
> TEACHER   "haec fātus." quid est hoc? quid dīcit Vergilius "haec fātus"?
>
> PUBLIUS   haec . . .
>
> TEACHER   quid est "haec"?
>
> LUCIUS   haec verba.
>
> TEACHER   ita vērō.
>
> PUBLIUS   haec verba dīxit et . . .

Meanwhile, the SLAVES in the corner are playing dice. There are cries of "Venus," "canis," "euge," "ēheu".

> TEACHER   optimē.
>
> CLASS   (*reciting*) haec fātus duplicem ex umerīs rēiēcit amictum . . .
>
> TEACHER   quid est "amictus"?
>
> DECIMUS   est lacerna.
>
> TEACHER   (*instructing the class*) iterum!
>
> CLASS   (*reciting*) haec fātus duplicem . . . (*etc.*)

As the class continues, loudly, a NEIGHBOUR uses Martial's words (see Appendix II) to yell a complaint.

> NEIGHBOUR   quid tibi nōbīscum est, lūdī scelerāte magister?

He continues as loudly as he can for as long as he can remember.

verba	*words*	amictum (duplicem)	*his (doubled) cloak*
"Venus"	*the best throw at dice*	lacerna	*cloak*
"canis"	*the worst throw at dice*	quid tibi est?	*what have you got?*
optimē	*well done!*	nōbīscum	(here) *against us*
ex umerīs	*from his shoulders*	lūdī . . . magister	*schoolmaster*
rēiēcit	*he flung back*	scelerāte	*wicked*

CLASS   (*reciting*) ex umerīs rēiēcit amictum et magnōs membrōrum artūs . . .

TEACHER   quid dīcit Vergilius?

PUBLIUS **flexes his arms, demonstrating his muscles.**

PUBLIUS   dīcit artūs, dīcit ossa, dīcit lacertōs.

DECIMUS   est āthlēta ingēns.

DECIMUS **demonstrates.**

PUBLIUS   ingentior.

PUBLIUS **also demonstrates.**

LUCIUS   est āthlēta ingentissimus.

Even LUCIUS gets involved. In the midst of this massive tumult—the DRUNKS are squabbling, the SIGNWRITERS are checking their words, the BREADSELLER can be heard, the CLASS noise and the NEIGHBOUR's complaints continue—MARCUS and PHILIPPUS, the two Christians, return. They must be allowed to be heard over the other noise.

PHILIPPUS   ecce! revēnimus. Chrīstus adest. nēmō nōs cōnspexit. nēmō nōs spectat. tūtī sumus, per Iēsum Chrīstum dominum nostrum.

MARCUS **makes a sign.**

MARCUS   deō grātiās agō.

There is a moment of sudden and eerie silence. After the silence, there are cries and movement from everybody but MARCUS and PHILIPPUS, who stand still and confident in the midst of chaos.

magnōs . . . artūs   *great joints*
membrōrum   *of his limbs*
dīcit   *is talking about*
ossa   *bones*
lacertōs   *muscles*

ALL	(*variously*) tremōrem sēnsī.
	fuge!
	abī!
	sollicitus
	fugite puerī!
	anxius
	quam celerrimē
	ēheu!
PHILIPPUS	est signum. Chrīstus ipse signum dedit. signum nōbīs dedit.
MARCUS	deō grātiās.

abī!	*go away!*	ipse	*himself*

PROPS

To provide, find, improvise or imagine.

The SIGNWRITERS must be able to write a sign. In reality a
large sheet of paper and a broad felt-tip pen (probably red)
would be most acceptable; it should *look* as though there
are a bucket of whitewash and a pot of paint, and as
though real brushes are being used on a wall.
Lamp
Ladder
"Papyrus sheet" which gives AEMILIUS his slogan
Baggages for MERCHANT
Tray of bread
School equipment in a "capsa" carried by SLAVE 3
PUBLIUS' breakfast (perhaps bought from the
    BREADSELLER?)
TEACHER's stick
"Something" for DECIMUS to drop
Dice for the SLAVES.

APPENDIX I

Pliny Letters VI.16

From a distance it was impossible to tell which mountain the cloud of smoke was rising from. (It turned out, of course, to be from Vesuvius.) As for its appearance, I can only describe it as being like a pine-tree. It went straight up into the air on a sort of long trunk, and then spread outward like a pine-tree's branches. This, I think, was because it had been pushed up by the early blast of air, and then was left to float when the force of the wind died away. Or perhaps it began to spread out when it became too heavy to rise any further. At times it looked white, but sometimes a blotched grey because of the earth and ashes in it.

My uncle . . . gave orders for a fast boat to be prepared, and offered me the chance of going with him. But I said that I preferred to study.(It so happened that he had given me some writing to do.) He steered a straight course right into the danger zone.

By now the ash was falling on the ships. It was getting hotter and thicker the nearer they came. Pumice stone too was falling, and bits of blackened rock, burned and broken off by the heat. Then suddenly they hit shallow water. The shore was blocked by rubble from the mountain.

Great spreading fires and tall flames were blazing all over Vesuvius. They seemed all the brighter in the darkness of night. To comfort people's fear, uncle kept on saying that these were bonfires left by the country people, or else their burning houses, now empty and deserted.

Frequent strong tremors were shaking the buildings, and they seemed to be rocking to and fro as though moving from their foundations. But in the open there was the fear of falling stones, however light and hollow they might be. My uncle thought it out carefully. They put cushions on their heads tied with strips of cloth, to protect themselves from the falling debris. It was daylight now everywhere else, but there the night was thicker and blacker than any real night, only lightened by all sorts of torches and lamps. They decided to go down to the shore to see for themselves. At close quarters it was clear that there was no chance of putting to sea. The waves were still high and unfriendly.

Pliny Letters VI.20

When my uncle left, I spent the rest of the day studying. Earth tremors had been happening for several days, but we hadn't worried. They are quite common there. But that night they were so strong that it felt as if the world was being shaken and turned upside down.

It was now just after dawn and still only faintly light. The buildings around us were shaking. If they collapsed, as seemed likely, we would be in danger. Even though we were out in the open, the space was narrow. That was when we decided to leave the town. A panic-stricken crowd followed us. In their terror they thought that to follow someone else's lead was the wisest thing to do. They pushed at our backs in a dense mob and swept us along.

Once away from the buildings we stopped. Fantastic and terrible things were all around us. For one thing, the carriages we had brought were running about all over the place, though the ground was quite level. Even when we wedged stones under the wheels, they wouldn't stand still. Then too we saw the sea being sucked into itself or pushed back, as you might say, by the tremors. The result was a wide expanse of beach with lots of sea creatures left high and dry on the sand. And over on the other side was the ugly black cloud, torn by quivering spirals of fire. It gaped open and showed great flaming shapes. They were like lightning flashes, but much bigger.

The Times 17th November 1868

THE ERUPTION OF VESUVIUS (from Our Own Correspondent)

On Saturday night a column of fire rose continually to a great height, obedient to an impulse which seemed to be given every two or three seconds. The light fell for some miles across the bay, and the waves by their undulations seemed to increase its intensity, giving it the appearance at times of a path inlaid with millions of flashing diamonds, at others of a path of solid fire. On Sunday night the side of the mountain was covered with fire, while the clouds which obscured the summit prevented us from seeing what was going on.

On Monday (that is yesterday) the clouds had cleared away, and looking from my window I witnessed, not a column, but a huge body of black smoke, rising, I should say, upwards of 2,000 feet in the air; it was not a rigid column, but through the glass appeared to be formed of innumberable circlets, rolling one over the other and mingling in their ascent.

The course of the lava, which flows most abundantly, was marked by a white smoke. Like the sluggish vapour from a marshy country, it rose slowly and lingered along the whole line, at points, however, ascending to a considerable elevation, suggesting the probability of another huge mouth having been opened. On such a scene it was that the sun shed its light, irradiating the eastern side of the column. No language I feel is adequate to a description of its glories. The whole mountain seemed on fire; the heavens seemed on fire; the sea was on fire; it was no longer a path of light that I saw, but a long extended sheet of fire.

APPENDIX II

Virgil is writing, in his grand style, a commentary on a boxing match. The preparations include the cruel leather boxing-thongs, tied on to fists to hurt more. The pose seems more upright and stiff than we expect nowadays, but the contrast between the boxers, and the techniques for enduring or avoiding the punches seem familiar.

haec fātus duplicem ex umerīs rēiēcit amictum
et magnōs membrōrum artūs, magna ossa lacertōsque
exuit atque ingēns mediā cōnsistit harēnā.
tum satus Anchīsā caestūs pater extulit aequōs
et paribus palmās ambōrum innexuit armīs.
cōnstitit in digitōs extemplō arrēctus uterque
bracchiaque ad superās interritus extulit aurās.
abdūxēre retrō longē capita ardua ab ictū
immiscentque manūs manibus pugnamque lacessunt,
ille pedum melior mōtū frētusque iuventā,
hic membrīs et mōle valēns; sed tarda trementī
genua labant, vastōs quatit aeger anhēlitus artūs.
multa virī nēquīquam inter sē vulnera iactant,
multa cavō laterī ingeminant et pectore vastōs
dant sonitūs, erratque aurēs et tempora circum
crēbra manus, dūrō crepitant sub vulnere mālae.
stat gravis Entellus nīsūque immōtus eōdem
corpore tēla modo atque oculīs vigilantibus exit.

Having spoken these (words), he threw back his double cloak;
and he bares the great joints of his limbs, his great bones and his
    upper arms
and stands, huge, in the middle of the arena.
Then the father (Aeneas), son of Anchises, carried out the
    equally matched boxing gloves
and laced up the hands of both of them in matched equipment.
Each of the two stood at once raised up onto his toes,
and unafraid lifted his arms to the breezes above.
They pulled their tall heads backwards far from the punching
and hands they mingle with hands, and bring on the fight.

That one is better in foot movement, and trusts his
   youthfulness;
this one is strong in his limbs and his massiveness: but as he
   wobbles, his slow
knees totter, an unhealthy breathlessness shakes his vast frame.
Many deadly punches the men aim at each other in vain,
they redouble many (punches) on their hollow ribs, and from
   their chest
they give off vast thumping-noises—many a hand misses the
   mark around their ears and temples,
their cheeks rattle under the tough punching.
Entellus stands heavy and motionless in the same stance;
with body(-movement) only and watchful eyes he avoids what-
   is-thrown-at-him.

haec	these (words)	lacessunt	provoke
fātus	having spoken	pedum mōtū	movement of feet
duplicem	double	melior	better
umerīs	shoulders	frētus	relying on
amictus	cloak	iuventā	youthfulness
membrōrum	limbs	mōle	in massiveness
artūs	joints	valēns	strong
ossa	bones	tarda	slow
lacertōs	upper arms	trementī	wobbling
exuit	bares	genua	knees
cōnsistit	stands	labant	totter
sātus Anchisā	son of Anchises	quatit	shakes
caestūs	boxing gloves	aeger	unhealthy
extulit	carried out, lifted	anhēlitus	breathlessness
paribus	equal, matched	nēquīquam	in vain
palmās	hands	vulnera	wounds, punches
ambōrum	both	laterī	side, ribs
innexuit	laced up	pectore	from the chest
in digitōs	on tip-toe	sonitūs	sounds
extemplō	at once	tempora	temples
arrēctus	raised up	crēbra manus	many a hand
uterque	each of two	crepitant	rattle
bracchia	arms	mālae	cheeks
interritus	unafraid	nīsū eōdem	in the same stance
aurās	breezes, air	immōtus	motionless
retrō	backwards	modo	only
ardua	high, tall	vigilantibus	watchful
ictū	blow	exit	avoids
immiscent	mingle		

quid tibi nōbīscum est, lūdī scelerāte magister,
    invīsum puerīs virginibusque caput?
nōndum cristāti rūpēre silentia gallī:
    murmure iam saevō verberibusque tonās.
tam grave percussīs incūdibus aera resultant,
    causidicum mediō cum faber aptat equō;
mītior in magnō clāmor furit amphitheātrō
    vincentī parmae cum sua turba favet.
vīcīnī somnum nōn tōtā nocte rogāmus:
    nam vigilāre leve est, pervigilāre grave est.
discipulōs dīmitte tuōs. vīs, garrule, quantum
    accipis ut clāmēs, accipere ut taceās?

lūdī magister	*schoolmaster*	aptat	*fits*
scelerāte	*wicked*	mītior	*more gently*
invīsum	*hateful*	furit	*rages*
caput (*here*) = *person*		vincentī	*winning*
nōndum	*not yet*	parmae	*small shield*
cristāti	*crested*	= *gladiators equipped with small shield*	
rūpēre = rūpērunt	*have broken*	turba	*crowd (of supporters)*
gallī	*cockerels*	vīcīnī	*neighbours*
murmure	*with shouting*	somnus	*sleep*
saevō	*savage*	tōtā nocte	*all night*
verberibus	*with beatings*	vigilāre	*to be awake*
tonās	*you thunder*	leve	*unimportant*
grave = graviter		pervigilāre	*to stay awake*
tam grave	*as heavily*	grave	*serious*
percussīs	*beaten*	discipulōs	*pupils*
incūdibus	*on anvils*	dīmitte	*send away*
aera	*bronzes (bronze statues)*	garrule	*chatterbox, constant talker*
resultant	*re-echo*	ut clāmēs	*so that you shout*
causidicum	*lawyer*	ut taceās	*so that you are quiet*
faber	*craftsman*		

What do you have to do with us, wicked schoolmaster,
a person hateful to boys and girls.
The crested cockerels have not yet broken the silence (of night):
already with savage shouting and beatings you are thundering.
Bronze (statues) re-echo just as heavily on beaten anvils,
    when a craftsman is fitting a (statue of a famous) lawyer on the
        middle of a (bronze) horse.
The shouting in the great amphitheatre rages more gently

when its own crowd (of supporters) supports "the small shield"
    when it is winning.
As neighbours we don't ask for sleep the whole night.
For to be awake is unimportant; to go on staying awake is
    serious.
Send your pupils away, you endless talker. Do you want
to take as much for being quiet as you take for shouting?

COMPLETE VOCABULARY

a

abit   goes *away:* abiit
accidit   *happened*
accipit   *accepts*
āctor: āctōrem   *actor*
ad   *to*
adest   *is here*
adiuvat   *helps*
adōrat   *worships*
aedificat   *builds*
aeger: aegrum   *sick, ill*
agit   *does, acts:* egit
  fābulam agit   *acts a play*
  grātiās agit   *gives thanks*
  negōtium agit   *does business, works*
  vītam agit   *lives*
agitat   *chases, hunts:* agitāvit
agnōscit   *recognises:* agnōvit
agricola   *farmer*
albus   *white*
alius   *other, another*
amat   *likes, loves*
amātor   *lover*
ambulat   *walks:* ambulāvit
amictus   *cloak*
amīcus   *friend*
amor   *love, desire*
amphitheātrum   *amphitheatre*
ancilla   *slave-girl, maid*
animal   *animal*
ante   *before*
anxius   *anxious*
arēna   *arena*
argentārius   *banker*
artus   *joint*
āthlēta   *athlete*
ātrium   *hall*
auctor: auctōrem   *creator*
audit   *hears:* audīvit
auris: aurem   *ear*

aut   *or*
  aut . . . aut   *either . . . or*
avia   *grandmother*

b

babae!   *I say! hey!*
baculum   *stick*
bellum   *war*
bene   *well*
benignus   *kind*
bēstia   *wild beast*
bibit   *drinks:* bibit

c

calamitās: calamitātem   *calamity, disaster*
callidus   *clever, cunning*
  callidissimus   *very clever*
candēlābrum   *lampstand*
canis: canem   *dog*
cantat   *sings*
capit   *takes*
capsārius   *book-box carrier*
caudex: caudicem   *blockhead, idiot*
cautē   *cautiously*
cavē, cavēte!   *beware!*
cavea   *seating area*
celeriter   *quickly*
  celerimmē   *very quickly*
  quam celerrimē   *as quickly as possible*
cēna   *dinner*
cēra   *wax, wax tablet*
cerasinus   *cherry-like*
certē   *for sure*
Chrīstiānus   *Christian*
cibus   *food*
cinis: cinerem   *ash*
cīvis: cīvem   *citizen*
clāmat   *shouts:* clāmāvit

clāmor: clāmōrem   *shout, uproar*
coccinus   *scarlet*
columba   *dove*
compōnit   *arranges*
cōnsilium   *plan, idea*
   cōnsilium capit   *makes a plan, has an idea*
cōnspicit   *catches sight of:* cōnspexit
cōnsūmit   *eats:* cōnsūmpsit
contendit   *hurries:* contendit
contrōversia   *debate*
corculum   *sweetheart*
crēdit   *trusts, believes, has faith in*
crūdēlis   *cruel*
cucurrit   *ran*
culīna   *kitchen*
cum   *with*
cupit   *wants*
cūr?   *why?*
cūrat   *looks after*
currit   *runs:* cucurrit

d

dat   *gives:* dedit
   fābulam dat   *puts on a play*
   poenam dat   *pays the penalty*
dē   *down from; about*
dealbātor   *whitener*
dedit   *gave, has given*
dēicit   *throws down*
dēlectat   *delights, pleases:* dēlectāvit
dēlet   *destroys:* dēlēvit
dēliciae   *darling*
dēnārius   *a denarius* (coin)
dēns: dentem   *tooth*
deus   *god*
dīcit   *says:* dīxit
discēdit   *departs, leaves:* discessit
discipulus   *pupil*
dīves: dīvitem   *rich*
dīxit   *said*
domina   *mistress, madam*
dominus   *master*
domus   *house, home*
dōnum   *present, gift*

dormit   *sleeps*
dūcit   *leads*
dulcis   *sweet, dear*
   dulcior   *dearer*
   dulcissimus   *dearest*
duplex: duplicem   *double*
dūrus   *hard*

e

ē, ex   *from, out of*
eam   *her, it*
ēbrius   *drunk*
ecce!   *see! look!*
effugit   *escapes:* effūgit
ēgit fābulam   *acted a play*
ego   *I*
ēheu!   *alas!*
emit   *buys*
eō   *I go*
eōs   *them*
ērādit   *rubs out, erases:* ērāsit
erat   *was*
est   *is*
et   *and*
euge!   *hurray!*
eum   *him, it*
ex   *out of, from*
exanimātus   *unconscious*
exspectat   *waits for*

f

fābula   *play, story*
facit   *makes, does:* fēcit
familia   *household*
fātus   *having spoken*
fēcit   *made, did*
fēlēs: fēlem   *cat*
fēlīx: fēlīcem   *lucky, happy*
fēmina   *woman*
ferōx: ferōcem   *fierce, ferocious*
fert   *brings, carries*
fessus   *tired*
festīnat   *hurries:* festīnāvit

fīlia *daughter*
fīlius *son*
flamma *flame*
flōs: flōrem *flower*
fōns: fontem *spring, source of water*
fortasse *perhaps*
frangit *breaks*
frāter: frātrem *brother*
fremit *roars*
frīgidus *cold*
fugit *runs away, flees*
fulvus *yellow*
fūr: fūrem *thief*
furcifer! *scoundrel!*
fūstis: fūstem *club*

g

gerit *wears*
gladiātor: gladiātōrem *gladiator*
gladius *sword*
Graecus *Greek*
grātiae *thanks*
  grātiās agit *gives thanks*

h

habet *has*
habitat *lives*
hae *these*
haec *this, these*
hanc *this*
haurit *drains, drinks up*
hercle! *by Hercules!*
heri *yesterday*
hī *these*
hic *this*
hīc *here*
hilaris *cheerful*
hoc *this*
hodiē *today*
homō: hominem *man*
horribilis *dreadful*
hortus *garden*
hūc *here, to here*
hunc *this*

i

iactat *juggles*
iam *now*
iamprīdem *a long time ago*
iānua *door*
ibi *there*
igitur *therefore, and so*
ignāvus *cowardly, lazy*
ille *that*
imitātor: imitātōrem *imitator*
immortālis *immortal*
in *in, on; into, onto*
incipit *begins*
induit *puts on*
īnfēlīx: īnfēlīcem *unlucky*
ingēns: ingentem *huge*
  ingentissimus *very large*
inimīcus *enemy*
inter *between, among*
intrat *enters:* intrāvit
invenit *finds:* invēnit
invītat *invites:* invītāvit
Iovi *to Jupiter*
ipse *himself*
īrātus *angry*
  īrātior *angrier*
  īrātissimus *very angry*
iste *that*
it *goes:* iit
ita *in this way*
ita vērō *yes*
iter *journey, progress*
iterum *again*
iubet *orders:* iussit
Iūppiter *Jupiter*
iūstus *just*
iuvenis: iuvenem *young man*

l

labōrat *works:* labōrāvit
lacerna *cloak*
lacertus *muscle*
lacrimat *weeps*
laetus *happy*

laetissimus   *very happy*
lanterna   *lamp*
lanternārius   *lamp-carrier*
larēs   *household gods*
laudat   *praises*
legit   *reads:* lēgit
lentē   *slowly*
leō: leōnem   *lion*
liber   *book*
līberāvit   *freed, set free*
līberī   *children*
lībertus   *freedman, ex-slave*
locus   *place*
longus   *long*
lūcet   *shines*
lūdit   *plays*
lūdus   *school*
lūna   *moon*
lupus   *wolf*

m

magis   *more*
magister   *schoolmaster*
magnus   *big, large, great*
maior   *bigger, larger, greater*
malus   *bad, evil*
manet   *remains, stays*
māter: mātrem   *mother*
mātrimōnium   *marriage*
maximē   *very much, most*
maximus   *very big, very large, very great,*
    greatest
mē   *me*
  mēcum   *with me*
medicus   *doctor*
medius   *middle*
melior   *better:* melius
membrum   *limb*
meus   *my, mine*
mihi   *to me, for me*
minimē!   *no!*
mīrābilis   *marvellous, strange, wonderful*
miser   *miserable, wretched*
  miserior   *more miserable*

miserrimus   *most miserable*
mittit   *sends:* mīsit
mōns: montem   *mountain*
moribundus   *almost dead, dying*
mortuus   *dead*
mox   *soon*
multus   *much, many*
mūrus   *wall*

n

nam   *for*
nārrat   *tells, relates:* nārrāvit
nāvigat   *sails:* nāvigāvit
nāvis: nāvem   *ship*
necat   *kills:* necāvit
necesse   *necessary*
nēmō: nēminem   *no one, nobody*
neptis   *granddaughter*
neque   *nor*
nescit   *does not know*
nihil, nīl   *nothing*
nōbīs   *to us, for us*
nōbīscum   *with us*
nōlō   *I do not want*
nōn   *not*
nōnne?   *surely . . . ?*
nōnvult   *does not want*
nōs   *we, us*
noster: nostrum   *our*
nox: noctem   *night*
nūbēs: nūbem   *cloud*
nūllus   *no*
num?   *surely . . . not?*
numquam   *never*
nunc   *now*

o

obdormīvit   *went to sleep*
obscūrus   *dark, gloomy*
  obscūrissimus   *very dark*
oculus   *eye*
odiōsus   *hateful*
offert   *offers*

omnis   *all*
optimē   *very well*
optimus   *very good, excellent, best*
ōrat   *beseeches*
os   *bone*
ōsculum   *kiss*
ostrea   *oyster*

p

paedagōgus   *pedagogue*
pānis: pānem   *bread*
pantomīmus   *mime actor*
parat   *prepares:* parāvit
parātus   *ready*
parvus   *small*
pater: patrem   *father*
pauper: pauperem   *poor*
  pauperior   *poorer*
  pauperrimus   *very poor*
pāvō: pāvōnem   *peacock*
pāx: pācem   *peace*
pecūnia   *money*
per   *through*
perīculōsus   *dangerous*
perīculum   *danger*
perterritus   *terrified*
pessimus   *worst, very bad*
pestis: pestem   *pest, scoundrel*
petit   *makes for, attacks, seeks:* petīvit
pila   *ball*
placet   *it pleases, suits*
plaudit   *applauds, claps:* plausit
plēnus   *full*
plumbeus   *made of lead*
pōculum   *wine-cup*
poena   *penalty, punishment*
Pompēiānus   *Pompeian*
pōnit   *puts:* posuit
populus   *nation, people*
portat   *carries:* portāvit
portus   *harbour*
poscit   *demands*
possum   *I can*
possumus   *we can*
possunt   *they can*

posuit   *placed, put up*
potest   *is able*
pretiōsus   *expensive, precious*
prīmus   *first*
prō   *in front of*
prōcēdit   *advances, proceeds*
prōcumbit   *falls flat*
prope   *near*
puella   *girl*
puer   *boy*
pugil: pugilem   *boxer*
pugna   *fight*
pugnāx: pugnācem   *aggressive, ready for
  a fight*
pugnat   *fights*
pulcher: pulchrum   *beautiful*
  pulchrior   *more beautiful*
  pulcherrimus   *very beautiful, very good
  looking*
pulsat   *hits, knocks at, thumps, punches*
pūnit   *punishes*

q

quaerit   *searches for, looks for:* quaesīvit
quam   *than, how*
  quam celerrimē   *as quickly as possible*
quantus!   *how big!*
quī   *who, which*
quid?   *what?*
quīnque   *five*
quīntus   *fifth*
quis?   *who?*
quō?   *where, where to?*
quō modō?   *how?*
quod   *because*
quoque   *also, too*

r

recipit   *takes*
rēicit   *throws back:* rēiēcit
rēs: rem   *thing*
respondet   *replies:* respondit
revenit, revēnit   *comes back, returns*

rhētor: rhētorem   *teacher*
rīma   *crack, chink*
rixa   *brawl*
rogat   *asks*
Rōmānus   *Roman*
rudēns   *rope*

S

sacerdōs: sacerdōtem   *priest*
sacrificium   *offering, sacrifice*
saepe   *often*
sagitta   *arrow*
salit   *leaps, jumps*
saltat   *dances*
salvē!   *hello!*
sanguinolentus   *bloody*
scālae   *ladder, set of steps*
scelerātus   *wicked*
scrībit   *writes:* scrīpsit
scrīptor: scrīptōrem   *signwriter*
secūris   *axe*
sed   *but*
sedet   *sits*
semper   *always*
senēscit   *grows old*
senex: senem   *old man*
sentit   *feels:* sēnsit
servat   *saves, looks after:* servāvit
servus   *slave*
sī   *if*
signum   *sign, seal, signal*
silentium   *silence*
silva   *wood*
sine   *without*
sollicitus   *worried, anxious*
sōlus   *alone, lonely*
somnus   *sleep*
sonus   *sound*
sordidus   *dirty*
spectat   *looks at, watches:* spectāvit
splendidus   *splendid*
stat   *stands*
statua   *statue*
stilus   *stylus, pen, stick*
stultus   *stupid*

stultior   *more stupid*
stultissimus   *very stupid*
suāvissimus   *sweetest*
subitō   *suddenly*
summus   *top*
superbus   *proud*
suspīrium   *heart-throb*
susurrat   *whispers*

t

tablīnum   *study*
tabula   *writing tablet*
tacet   *is silent, is quiet*
tamen   *however*
tandem   *at last*
tantus   *so great, so big*
tardus   *late*
tē   *you (singular)*
   tēcum   *with you (singular)*
templum   *temple*
tenet   *holds*
terra   *ground, land*
terret   *frightens*
tertius   *third*
testāmentum   *will*
theātrum   *theatre*
thermae   *baths*
tibi   *to you (singular), for you*
timet   *is afraid, fears*
titulus   *notice, slogan*
toga   *toga*
trādit   *hands over*
tragoedia   *tragedy*
tremit   *trembles, shakes:* tremuit
tremor: tremōrem   *trembling, tremor*
triclīnium   *dining-room*
trīstis   *sad*
tū   *you (singular)*
tum   *then*
tūtus   *safe*
tuus   *your, yours*

u

ubi   *where, when*

ubi?   *where?*
ululāvit   *howled*
umbra   *shadow, ghost*
umerus   *shoulder*
unde?   *where from?*
ūnus   *one*
urbs: urbem   *city*
ūrit   *burns*
ut   *as*
uxor: uxōrem   *wife*

V

vāgīvit   *cried, wailed*
valdē   *very much, very*
valē   *goodbye*
validus   *strong*
  validior   *stronger*
vēnātor: vēnātōrem   *hunter*
venēnum   *poison*
venia   *favour, forgiveness*
venit   *comes:* vēnit
verberat   *strikes, beats:* verberāvit
verbum   *word*
vērum   *truth*
vestīmenta   *clothes*

vexat   *annoys*
via   *street*
vīcīnus   *neighbour*
victima   *victim*
videt   *sees:* vīdit
vīlla   *house, villa*
vincit   *wins, defeats:* vīcit
vīnum   *wine*
vir   *man, husband*
virgae   *bundle of rods (for beating)*
viridis   *green*
vīs   *you want* (singular)
vīta   *life*
vituperat   *blames, curses*
vīvus   *alive*
vōbīs   *to you* (plural), *for you*
vōbīscum   *with you* (plural)
vocat   *calls:* vocāvit
volō   *I want*
volumus   *we want*
vōs   *you* (plural)
vōx: vōcem   *voice*
vult   *wants*
vultis   *you want* (plural)
vultus   *face*